At Face Value

By C. J. McNaspy, S.J.
Preface by Walker Percy
Afterword by David A. Boileau

WIPF & STOCK · Eugene, Oregon

Wipf and Stock Publishers
199 W 8th Ave, Suite 3
Eugene, OR 97401

At Face Value
A Biography of Father Louis J. Twomey, S.J.
By McNaspy, C. J., S.J. and Kammer, Fred, S.J.
Copyright © 1978 Loyola University New Orleans All rights reserved.
Softcover ISBN-13: 978-1-6667-4295-4
Hardcover ISBN-13: 978-1-6667-4296-1
eBook ISBN-13: 978-1-6667-4297-8
Publication date 3/21/2022
Previously published by Loyola University of the South, 1978

This edition is a scanned facsimile of the original edition published in 1978.

Preface

There are special reasons why a biography of Louis Twomey is timely now. One is that a particularly good, brave and gifted man always needs to be remembered, especially in his own country and in the South he served so well. Something is wrong when a man like Father Twomey is known better in Calcutta than in New Orleans where most of his life work was done. Something is wrong when a young Jesuit at Loyola in New Orleans wants to know "Who was this Twomey they named Twomey House after?"

But there is another reason, more peculiar to the times, why Louis Twomey needs to be rescued from the flux of years. It has to do with the extraordinary acceleration of change in virtue of which the burning issues of the day lose their drama and immediacy, not after a century or so as they used to, but now in a matter of a decade. Thus, while one remembers all too well how misunderstood Father Twomey was in the 1950s and 60s, change moves upon change so swiftly that ten years from now one might not even be able to understand the misunderstanding.

For what one remembers is Father Twomey being called a "Communist agitator" by more than a few Catholic laymen and even some of his fellow priests. It is enough to make you smile and shake your head now, but it wasn't funny then. Because one remembers also that this same Father Twomey used to anathematize Communism in his Loyola classes in terms so uncompromising and evangelical as to embarrass a good Republican in these days of *detente*.

But of course what stuck in the craw of so many Southerners was not his pronouncements about Marxism, pro or con, but his unflinching stand on social justice, justice for the working man but above all justice for the black man. Change accelerates, the past hastens ever more swiftly into oblivion, and it is all too easy to forget that Negroes had to sit in the rear of streetcars only a few short years ago and couldn't get into Audubon Park at all—and that the city closed the pool rather than have black kids in it. Better no kids at all.

Nor does it seem now a remarkable achievement for Twomey to have integrated his Institute of Human Relations at Loyola in 1950—even though it was the first instance of integrated education on a campus in the Deep South since Reconstruction. So what? the reader is apt to think now. Would it not in fact have been downright unnatural that an institute about human relations shouldn't have been integrated from the beginning? Once again an effort of memory—and a certain honesty about one's own reactions—is required to capture the flavor of the times and the shock, outraged shock to the conservatives, but shock to us too, yes, secret shock to us self-styled moderates: what's this? a "Negro" actually at Loyola? in the classroom? sitting at cafeteria tables? Wasn't Twomey rushing things a bit? Maybe he was, but time was rushing too and nobody was surprised when, a few years later, a Negro student was elected president of the student body. It is pleasant to know that Father Twomey lived to see this.

Perhaps the most engaging quality of Father McNaspy's biography is his success in portraying his subject not as standard hagiography but, as he says, "with warts and all." If indeed there were warts, they serve mainly to make him one of us, for we recognize them as our own. It was particularly comforting to me to learn that Twomey as late as 1943 still wondered whether the difficulties of Negroes might be traced to the curse of Ham. Since most of us Southerners, I at least, were born and raised staunch segregationists, it might have been edifying but also somehow depressing to have read that Louis Twomey had sprung from Tampa fully armed for doing battle against Florida segregationists and the exploitation of workers in the cigar factory. No, it is a relief to learn that he cared more about sports, that he had an awful temper playing baseball and that he was good enough to be offered a contract by the Washington Senators.

A personal note: How does one remember him? Strange, but though I saw him more than a few times and under quite different circumstances, it is always a particular image of him that comes to mind when I think of him. He is sitting on a low sofa in my house where he had come for supper before speaking to the student body of a local prep school. He is a lank man; pale, long face, yet fit; big hands, bony knees riding high and a bit awkward like a Georgia parson come to pay a call in the parlor; chain-smoker, big hoarse voice (one wondered whether it was the cigarettes or the public speaking). Somehow he gives the effect of wearing the blackest properest clerical blacks I ever saw. Perhaps it is also his very dark hair neatly combed from low above his dark eyes. In a word, today's word, he was as square a priest as one can imagine. And of course he was. It was 1964, the time of Vatican II but the only "new things" he cared about were *Rerum Novarum* and the old social encyclicals of the last century which had not yet caught up with the South and were "rerum novarum" indeed.

Memory tricks and contradicts. My daughter sang and played the guitar for him and remembers him as being jovial; he laughed a lot and talked about Joan Baez. My wife remembers him as being intense, dour and fiery-eyed. True, he refused a cocktail and preferred to talk about the principle of subsidiarity. Hm. He talked about Communism and *Quadrigesimo Anno* and why it was that the best and possibly only defense against Communism was social justice based on Christian principles. So? Not even politicians argue with that now. So what more needs to be said except that surely it was simply part and parcel of the times, the crazy sixties of assassinations and school children cheering news of Kennedy's death that Twomey of all people should have been called a Communist agitator.

Of course he was all these things one remembers, dour and jovial, intense and affable, smiling and fiery-eyed, "conservative" and "liberal" in the particular reading of these peculiar words at the time. Square? yes, and agitator? yes indeed. He knew how to shake people up.

The only thing I remember about the speech he gave was the first thing he said—perhaps a typical Twomey gambit (I don't know what position he played in baseball but he talked like an angry short-stop). He stood up and gazed around at the assembled students and faculty and said in his big hoarse orator's voice something like: "Why don't I see a single black face here?" Shocked silence. Outraged silence. Murmurings. Stirrings. Chair scrapings. Students rose angrily to defend, justify. After all it was only 1964 and that was a long time ago.

He was a good man to have around and there were too few like him. As much as anyone he pricked and wakened the conscience of the South. And if the South's conscience is now more responsive than the rest of the nation's, he surely had something to do with it. He doesn't need us to remember him now, but we need to.

Walker Percy

Foreword

The choice of a title for this life of Fr. Louis Twomey was not the hardest task facing the two authors. But it was not easy.

One title that a friend suggested was "El Divino Impaciente." We had no difficulty with the fact that it had already been used for José-Maria Pemán's play about Francis Xavier. For Lou Twomey was always in a hurry, impatient, perhaps "divinely" so. Much like Francis Xavier he was both driven and driving. His passion was singly that of social justice.

But a title should normally be in the vernacular, and we saw no way of translating "El Divino Impaciente" into adequate English. The title of Pemán's play in English is "Saint in a Hurry," which fits the canonized Xavier but seems not quite so apt for Lou Twomey. This little biography is meant to be neither a panegyric nor a brief for the canonization process. Our aim is more modest: a portrait, warts and all, which we hope will be recognizable to Lou's many friends and a truthful introduction to those who know him only by name.

At Face Value, as a title, was lifted from a conference that always proved a high point during spiritual retreats given by Lou Twomey. This he called "Taking Christ at Face Value." This title in turn was taken from the story of Chaplain Joseph Timothy O'Callahan, awarded the Congressional Medal of Honor for his heroism during World War II on the carrier *Franklin*. In his autobiographical account, *I Was Chaplain on the Franklin* (Macmillan, 1956), Father O'Callahan remarked almost parenthetically "All my life I had been trained to take Christ's teachings at face value." (p. 88)

Somehow the phrase seemed to fit Lou Twomey himself and to serve as an epitome of his aspirations. Further, he was the sort of person who could be taken at face value. Even those farthest from sharing his passion for social justice had to admit that you could trust Lou. There was a transparency about him that was totally undiplomatic, uncontrived, some might say unjesuitical.

A word now about our division of labor. The ground work of research was done by John R. Payne in preparation for a dissertation in American Studies presented to the University of Texas at Austin. Years of probing into files of documents and letters were added to hundreds of hours of taped oral interviews with just about everyone who ever worked with Lou Twomey.

John Payne pressed his former teacher, C. J. McNaspy, into collaboration. While most of the research is Payne's, the collaborator is responsible for organization and composition. As a close personal friend of Lou's he undertook the task with some alacrity, yet conscious of the perils of subjectivity. Whenever the pronoun "I" appears in the text, it is McNaspy, not Payne, expressing himself.

The authors are grateful to hundreds of helpers in their undertaking. To name them all would seem inappropriate, if not impossible. Obvious exceptions, however, are the distinguished novelist Walker Percy and David Boileau, Lou's successor as director of the Institute of Human Relations at Loyola University, New Orleans, who made publication possible.

We feel that a life of Lou Twomey is timely. A number of his contemporaries and associates are no longer living and it becomes somewhat urgent to do oral history before it is too late. At the same time, in the seven years since Lou's death a generation of young students and brother Jesuits has come along who know him only as a name. The other day, in fact, a young Jesuit asked: "Who was this Twomey they named Twomey House after?" It seemed time, indeed.

Even more shocking, perhaps, was the *lacuna* we observed in the recent *Supplement* to the *New Catholic Encyclopedia* (1967-1974). Rich as this volume is in biographical articles on important American Catholics deceased during those eight years, Louis J. Twomey's name appears nowhere. This served us as yet another prod.

Happily, just before we decided to embark on this biography, one of Lou Twomey's close friends and associates completed a work that should be read in close conjunction with this: *One-Man Research: Reminiscences of a Catholic Sociologist*, by Joseph H. Fichter. Especially during the critical years from 1947 to 1960, while both were at Loyola University in New Orleans, they were frequent collaborators and the Fichter reminiscences provide indispensable background for a Twomey biography.

Table of Contents

Preface 3

Foreword 7

Chapter 1
    Father Louis J. Twomey 11

Chapter 2
    Early Life 21

Chapter 3
    Labor 39

Chapter 4
    Communism 61

Chapter 5
    Race 71

Chapter 6
    Evaluation 81

Chapter 7
    Death 89

Afterword 93

Father Louis J. Twomey, S.J. and Walker Percy

Chapter 1

"Oh, you're from New Orleans. Do you happen to know Father Lou Twomey?"

I chuckled and replied: "Very, very well. Why do you ask?"

"Because he's very much responsible for our work here in Calcutta. When I was a seminarian in Australia I always read his bulletin *Christ's Blueprint for the South*. It fired me with the desire to do something. When I saw Calcutta and the work of Mother Teresa among the poorest of the poor, I felt that this was what I was called to do. When you see Father Twomey, do tell him."

I did, in fact, reach New Orleans in time to tell the story to Lou Twomey. He was in the hospital, nearer death than most of us realized. Several of his friends were celebrating Mass for him, and I felt that the right time to tell him about Brother Andrew in Calcutta was during the homily. Lou smiled, dropped his head, and breathed audibly: "Thank God!"

Aware as I had long been of Lou Twomey's influence on the social consciousness of his brother Jesuits in America, I was struck (as doubtless he must have been at the thought of this influence reaching the antipodes. During a meeting of missiologists in Hong Kong, I had been urged by several Australians to stop in Calcutta to see Brother Andrew (whose previous name had been Ian Travers-Ball). I had heard, of course, of Mother Teresa's work there—even before Malcolm Muggeridge's biography of her, *Something Beautiful for God*, appeared, mentioning Andrew's work too—but had not previously known of Andrew. His community of Indian brothers now numbers over 200, and their work has extended beyond Calcutta. Recently, when Brother Andrew was in this country, he made a sort of pilgrimage to New Orleans, where most of Lou Twomey's work was centered.

Loyola University in New Orleans became, in fact, the locus—perhaps more precisely the springboard—of Lou's most creative years. In 1947 he arrived there to begin his work and was allotted a spartan ten-by-thirty-foot office and an even more spartan twenty-dollars-a-month budget. He borrowed a typewriter from his friend Father Joseph H. Fichter, S.J., then chairman of the sociology department. (This was the year before Fichter did his important sociological study of a New Orleans Catholic parish, published by the University of Chicago Press and titled *The Dynamics of a City Church*. The vicissitudes of this seminal work and an account of Fichter's life of research are fully given in his autobiographical study: *One-Man Research: Reminiscences of a Catholic Sociologist*.)

Lou then founded what he called the Institute of Industrial Relations, later to be known as the Institute of Human Relations. Moral backing came from Archbishop Joseph F. Rummel, who sent a letter to the Catholic clergy encouraging their attendance at Institute courses. The mayor of New Orleans, de Lesseps S. Morrison, congratulated the president of Loyola, Father Thomas J. Shields, S.J., on the Institute's establishment, stating that it was "a major step in the direction of lasting industrial peace, when representatives of labor and management sit down together to discuss objectively the improvement of their relationship." Vastly expanded, the Institute continues its work under the direction of Father David A. Boileau. David Boileau, John Payne, and I were happy to welcome Brother Andrew on the occasion of his visit to New Orleans and the Institute.

No less symbolic of the spread of Twomey's inspiration, and even more practically significant, was the major letter of November 1, 1967 addressed to Jesuits throughout the world by their superior general Pedro Arrupe, S.J., "On the Interracial Apostolate." While the letter represented the official thought of Father Arrupe, it was an open secret that much of its content and composition had been provided by Father Twomey in collaboration with an old friend and associate, Fr. William Kenealy, S.J., of Boston. All of Lou's close friends recognized in this solemn document the peak of his life's work. What for many years had been his personal vision and effort became explicitly furthered at the highest level of the religious order to which he belonged.

Not that this recognition, which came shortly before his death, was the only time Lou's work had been shown official Jesuit appreciation. Back on October 13, 1958, Father Arrupe's predecessor, John Baptist Janssens, S.J., wrote him a warm letter of congratulations on the tenth anniversary of his monthly bulletin, *Christ's Blueprint for the South*. "Your vision has been proven correct," wrote Father Janssens. He concluded with the promise of prayers that the *Blueprint* would "continue to keep before Jesuits a due sense of personal commitment to the all-important Social Apostolate and prevent exaggerated complacence in the task thus far accomplished." Complacence was the last pitfall in the world ever to face Lou himself, always divinely impatient and eager to get on with the work to be done.

The *Blueprint* (now titled *Blueprint for the Christian Reshaping of Society* and edited by Fr. David A. Boileau may well have been Lou Twomey's most lasting and effective single contribution. Its first issue was dated November 15, 1948—a six-page, single spaced typewritten copy, in much the same format as is used today. Only fifty copies of this first issue went out to Jesuits of the South. By 1958 over 2,000 copies were being sent monthly to Jesuits throughout the United States and 44 foreign countries. By the time Lou died, in 1969, more than 3,000 copies went out every month. These twenty-one years of consistent publication by a single person, to a select but significant readership, would alone make Lou Twomey an exceptional voice in the annals of journalism. The response is reflected in the collection of over 40,000 letters exchanged between Lou and readers around the world and now kept at Loyola. Little wonder that Peter Henriot, founder of the Center for Concern in Washington, judged that "he was the single most effective force in shaping the social conscience of younger Jesuits."

This is not to suggest that Lou Twomey's work and influence were principally intramural, within his religious family. While he sensed the value of working with his Jesuit brothers, in the belief that they would, as teachers, preachers and retreat directors, exert pressure for needed social change, he spent most of his energy working with lay people. Even as a writer, apart from his wide lecturing, Lou was active particularly among youth. An important vehicle he found was *The Queen's Work,* a magazine directed largely toward youth in Sodalities—religious clubs for social and service projects. In the decade between 1951 and 1961, Lou wrote more than fifty articles on social topics in this magazine, reaching a readership of tens of thousands.

Associated with *The Queen's Work* were week-long summer sessions known as the Summer School of Catholic Action (SSCA). These institutes were largely the inspiration of Fr. Daniel Lord, S.J., (1888-1955), remembered by Catholics who were in school during the thirties, forties and fifties as a most dynamic, charismatic influence on youth. Father Lord attracted teachers for these summer sessions covering many facets of Christian life (I personally taught courses in liturgy and liturgical music back in the forties).

From 1947, Lou Twomey was a powerful voice in the SSCA for almost twenty years, reaching thousands of young teachers and future leaders. The SSCA itinerary for 1956 may be taken as typical of other summers: New York City, Chicago, Cleveland, New Orleans, St. Paul, San Antonio and Worcester, Mass. Thus, in the course of two decades Lou Twomey achieved the widest exposure as a lecturer, over and above his continuous writing. It should not be overlooked that Dan Lord, who strongly inspired Lou Twomey, was (from 1943-1947) director and catalyst of the Institute of Social Order (under national Jesuit auspices) and for some years editor of *Social Order* magazine, to which Lou was a frequent contributor, and later editor.

"I met Lou during the SSCA, summer of 1954," reminisces Neil Hurley, author and social-communications expert in Chile. "In his gruff voice, sweetened by a touch of southern drawl, he said: 'Neil, how are yuh?' At the same time he firmly pulled my clasped hand toward his heart. I have met thousands of people since then, but nobody made the authentic impression of personal interest in me as

Father Vincent O'Connell, S.M. and Father Twomey

did Lou. As delicate as he was toward others, he was direct in his attacks on groups which were morally blinded. He sensed what our 'liberation theologians' would later call 'institutional violence.' He was God's draughtsman, who dedicated his life on behalf of Christ's blueprint for South America as well as the south, and indeed for the shrinking planet that we call Spaceship Earth."

This sort of tribute from social thinkers on every continent could be repetitiously multiplied into a litany. I find it typical of the response given by people who came into Lou's world ten, twenty or thirty years ago. It suggests, too, that even contacts that might have been thought ephemeral created impressions that have perdured. Neil Hurley's memory of the warmth and palpable authenticity noted in Lou Twomey I have heard expressed again by hundreds of persons interviewed.

Hurley's mention of South America suggests yet another Twomey involvement, one that particularly occupied his last years. We have a letter from him, dated January 21, 1959, to Marco Aurelio Merida, Minister of Public Education of Guatemala, expressing satisfaction that he (Twomey) "was able to be of some help in exploring particularly the possibility of promoting the credit union movement in Guatemala." At about this time, Lou conceived "An Educational Plan for Social Institutions in Central America, Panama and the Dominican Republic" (the title of a feasibility survey). This evolved, as we shall see later, into an Inter-American Center "to train younger leadership groups in the ideas, ideals, tactics, and techniques of building democratic, social institutions . . . to create a society in which the dignity of the human person is acknowledged, protected, and respected."

The Inter-American Center functioned from 1964 to 1971 and included an average of 250 students each year. At first attendants were from Central American countries, most of them unfamiliar with the complexity of highly industrialized economic society. Gradually, however, students came from such countries as Brazil and Colombia, widening the Center's scope. During the first year alone 84 lecturers from the New Orleans academic and civic communities participated in the Center's programs, drawn by the contagious zest of organizer Lou Twomey.

"If Father Twomey is ever called 'blessed,' it'll come from Latin America rather than North America," stated Twomey's former assistant director at the Center, B. Raynal ("Ray") Ariatti. Ray had accompanied Lou on several trips to Central America and returned to the Congress of alumni of the Center, held in Panama City the year following Lou's death. Among these socially sensitized leaders, Lou's name was held in high benediction and his portrait warmly venerated. Beneath the Latin rhetoric one sensed an almost unprecedented gratitude and dedication.

This is hardly to suggest that Lou Twomey was unappreciated elsewhere nor that tributes came in only posthumously. A year before his death he received an unexpected letter of congratulations on the success of his Institute of Human Relations. It came from the American ambassador to New Zealand, John F. Henning, who had just met representatives of American university presidents, Nathan Pusey of Harvard and Herbert Longenecker of Tulane. The Ambassador had inquired of Dr. Longenecker how his old friend Lou Twomey was, and the report had elicited a welcome gratuitous letter (preserved in the Louis Twomey Collection, Document Center at Loyola University in New Orleans; most of the documents referred to *passim* are contained in this Collection, and precise references may be found in John Payne's dissertation).

At this time, too, came a heartening tribute from novelist Walker Percy. In his "New Orleans *Mon Amour*" in the September, 1968, issue of *Harper's*, Dr. Percy described the glamour and squalor of New Orleans, singling out Father Twomey as the "one man hereabouts" who has done more than any other "to translate Catholic social principles into meaningful action." Among the accomplishments mentioned were "his valuable services in labor-management conciliation," the Institute of Human Relations, and his assistance "in its campaign for social justice for the Negro and in the education of the unskilled."

Two years earlier unexpected civic accolade was conferred by the city where he did most of his work and where he was judged most controversial. On the evening of October 1, 1966, in the Seafarers International Union building, New Orleans, a testimonial dinner brought together a galaxy of important citizens, lay and clerical, black and white, laborers and executives, and such government leaders as the late United States Congressman Hale Boggs. The master of ceremonies, Lindsay Williams, Vice-President of the Seafarers International Union, read telegrams of congratulations from President Lyndon Johnson, Vice-President Hubert Humphrey, George Meany, Walter Reuther and other important figures. A leading black Baptist minister, A. L. Davis, thanked God for Louis Twomey, since "his life reveals Thy majesty." Rabbi Julian Feibelman urged Lou "to remember this great evening when the city poured out to show that you are loved and honored and respected and admired." I was not able to be present at the banquet, but I recall the gratitude Lou felt as he modestly told me of the event and surprise he experienced at this support. One who was there recalls Lou's tears at the applause of several hundred guests.

It need hardly be said that this moment of glory was exceptional in Lou's life and did nothing to take away his pressing sense of urgency. "C. J., I'm worried!" was the sort of greeting that his friends got used to. Occasionally one would playfully get the first word in: "What's the crisis today, Lou?" He would smile, then shake his head and start answering your question quite literally. He seemed never unworried.

Amid his controversial activity there was no dearth of recognition. President Lyndon Johnson appointed him in 1964 to the National Citizens Committee for Community Relations. He was also a member of the 10-man National Manpower Advisory Committee of the U.S. Department of Labor and the Department of Health, Education and Welfare. On the national level, he was one of the 15-man Citizens Advisory Committee on Civil Rights for the U.S. Department of Agriculture and served on the Congressional Committee for the Administration of Training Programs of HEW. In his honor a tree was planted in Israel.

Locally, Louisiana Governor John McKeithen in 1967 appointed Lou to a 9-man Labor-Management Commission of inquiry, and New Orleans Mayor Victor H. Schiro in the same year named him a member of the advisory of the committee of Delgado College.

After his death, unsurprisingly, eulogies began to be multiplied. While the New Orleans secular press, as might have been expected, made no editorial comment, M. F. Everett, editor of the *Clarion-Herald* dedicated a lengthy column in praise of a "Truly Great Leader." The same newspaper's leading columnist, Mel Leavitt, lauded him as a "Giant Human Rights Leader," quoting Lou rather typically: "You can look up at the stars and still keep both feet on the ground; we've got to do that; we've got to do that."

An esteemed lawyer, John Nelson, Jr. (whose work with Lou we shall treat later), gave this balanced tribute: "He understood the weaknesses and the strengths in people, and believed in the decency he felt lies within every fellow man. He constantly spoke of the dignity of the individual and he sought progress not through confrontation politics, but through reason, action, and compassion. He hoped until the end that something in us would pull us into the future."

Funerals are often bedizened with rhetorical exaggerations. Fortunately the person chosen to deliver Lou's funeral address was a serious scholar, then Academic Vice-President of Loyola University, Thomas H. Clancy, S.J., who spoke in measured terms that should be read more than once:

" 'Do not forget what I said to you: no servant can be greater than his master. They will persecute you just as they have persecuted me . . . and they will treat you thus because you bear my name.' These words are taken from Christ's farewell address to his apostles as recorded in St. John's Gospel.

"In its liturgy for the dead, the Church prays that the angels will receive the departed soul and that the martyrs welcome it. The word 'martyr' has been vulgarized. People apply the term to themselves because they have to wait in traffic or in the anteroom of the bishop's office. The original meaning of martyr was simply 'witness'. The true martyrs are those who discover the hard truth of Jesus' prophecy that no one can honestly witness to truth in this wicked world without suffering. Father Twomey learned that lesson, but he always found it difficult to accept. The most striking paradox of his life was that such a kind man would have been embroiled most of his life in controversy.

"Father Louis Twomey was a fighter all his life, but he never spoiled for a fight. One of the things he found hardest to understand was why people fought with him. It was all so clear to him what he must do, what he must say. Like the prophets of the Old Testament who were summoned unwillingly by God to bring his message to a stiff-necked generation, Father Twomey spread the gospel message almost unwillingly to a people who in large part were unwilling, or not yet ready to hear it, and he found suffering. He found opprobrium.

"It takes nothing away from the wonderful work Father Twomey did in education to say that he did his greatest work here at Loyola in the Institute of Human Relations and the Institute of Industrial Relations during the last 22 years of his life. These institutions enshrined his dream of making a better life for the children of God, his dream of making sure that every man—no matter what his station in life or what his color—was treated as befitted the dignity of creatures stamped with the image of God. Father Twomey did not find this inspiration by means of giant intellectual effort. The inspiration for his life was grounded, yes, in the Papal teachings, in the findings of modern social science and in the social realities of the South which he loved. All of that is true, but throughout his life the catalyst of his convictions was prayer.

"Which brings us to the second paradox of Father Twomey's life.

He was a modern priest attached to old-fashioned piety. Many priests who preach of the social gospel, who prophesy hard things for men of wealth and power and small minds, are often criticized because they neglect the traditional forms of piety and religious devotion. None of the men, either of good will or bad will, who opposed and criticized Father Twomey during his long life could say that of him. To the very end his piety was that which he learned at his mother's knee. He was a man who prayed the rosary to his last day on earth, who found nourishment and comfort in the devotion to the Sacred Heart. He was always and evidently a priest and man of God. One remembers how he used to gather his staff in the Institute of Human Relations together to recite the Angelus at noon. And when he went on automobile trips there were always prayers, and not short prayers, for a safe trip. Whether he was in Washington or in Baton Rouge or in a convention or giving a speech, Father Twomey was unmistakably a priest. His life of prayer enabled him to see with a clarity denied to the scholar and the intellectual the real problems of our city and state and nation.

"This brings us to the third paradox of Father Twomey's life: a humble man of God always conscious of the divine dimension of human affairs, he achieved secular greatness and became one of the most influential men of his time. I do not say this lightly or in the spirit of exaggerated praise that is pardonable in funeral discourses. Any historian who studies the history of post-World-War II America must reckon with the figure of Louis J. Twomey. He was one of the original band of labor priests who had a profound influence on the trade union movement in this country. He saw the tragedy of racism in the South, the nation and the world, and combatted it manfully. Through his vast publications and through the literally thousands of letters he wrote to people throughout the world, through the hundreds of visitors he entertained and educated to the ignominies and realities as well as the good points of the South, he was perhaps among the six or seven best known priests in America.

"I remember how often people in England, France and Germany asked me, when they discovered I was from New Orleans, "Do you know Father Twomey?" And those who have traveled more widely than I have told me of the same thing happening in India, Taiwan, and the Latin-American countries.

"At the end of his life he was instrumental in starting a program for Central American citizens. It was typical of him that the program was designed not for diplomats or for intellectuals but for the ordinary working people of Central America. The General of the Society of

Jesus, Father Pedro Arrupe, followed the example of his predecessors and exhibited a close interest in Father Twomey's work and recommended it as a model to Jesuits working in social apostolates in all parts of the world, especially in the underdeveloped countries.

"Father Twomey had a truly Christian internationalism, but he was a great patriot. None of the hard things said about him hurt him more than the aspersions cast on his loyalty to this country. And yet there are not two dozen people in this land to whome America owes more than it does to Father Twomey. Our nation's presidents recognized that and honored him, at least in the last ten years of his life.

"President Eisenhower appointed him to the State Advisory Council of the National Civil Rights Commission. President Johnson appointed him to the National Citizens Committee for Community Relations. He was a personal friend of long standing of many of the nation's economic and political leaders.

"We must speak of this because Father Twomey rarely did. He was never a name dropper, and it is perhaps difficult for us who lived close to him, who knew the foibles reflected in the hundreds of 'Father Twomey stories' to realize his national and international stature.

"I could say much more. All I have said up to now is simply a reflection of conversations which have taken place since Wednesday in the Jesuit dining room, at the wake, and over the telephone with the many persons who have called. One question many ask is: what will happen to Father Twomey's work? It is difficult to imagine how we will carry on without him, but we would be unfaithful to his memory if we did not resolve to do so. He has shown us the way.

"We have lost a great man, a great priest, a great Jesuit, a great American. Let us pray for the soul of this courageous crusader. Let us pray for this city and this Southland that he loved so well and that he worried about and argued with so constantly, and let us pray for this nation and for all the people with whom he felt an instinctive bond, the poor, the downtrodden, the same people in whose company our Divine Savior was found throughout his life. Amen."

Chapter 2
EARLY LIFE

Had Lou Twomey died just after his ordination (June 21, 1939) at the age of 33, one of his brother Jesuits would have written a traditional obituary note to be read by several hundred other Jesuits in the South. It would have sounded like many another sketch and ended with regrets that a person of such spirit and spirituality had been lost to his friends and great promises left unfulfilled.

For up to this time there was little to suggest what these promises might specifically hold. Like many another priest, Jesuit or otherwise, he came from a fine, solidly Christian family. He was a class leader, both academically and athletically. He had been respected by his peers and loved by them during high school, college and his years of seminary training in the Society of Jesus. Much the same could have been written of many of his conferees.

This chapter, accordingly, holds no startling revelations. The material we have laboriously accumulated from scattered remaining letters and a number of interviews might possibly contain grist for some psychiatric mill. Since neither of the authors can claim any advanced training in analysis, in all fairness we serve warning that the sketch of Lou's young life will be narrative, with little beyond the barest hint at interpretation. Even a Lytton Strachey, for all his skill at digging up titillating tidbits, could hardly have found the young Twomey an engaging subject for one of his biographies, though he might have thought him altogether Victorian. We hope not to be too pretentious if we subscribe to Strachey's affirmed intention: "To preserve a becoming brevity—a brevity which excludes everything that is redundant and nothing that is significant . . . to lay bare the facts of the case, as (we) understand them."

Louis Joseph Twomey was born October 5, 1905, in Tampa, Florida. He was the third child and second son of Timothy J. Twomey and Annie Savarese Twomey. His mother had been born and reared in Georgia. Her father and uncles had fought on the Confederate side

Father Twomey as a young scholastic visiting Loyola University

during the Civil War. Later, when Lou was vigorously involved in social justice for blacks, he could always point to his strong Southern roots, exploding any charge that he was a damn yankee.

At that time Tampa had a population of just over 16,000, with fewer than 2,000 Catholics. Inevitably, this meant a strong feeling of identity and even militancy. During his childhood and adolescence Lou knew the bigotry of the Ku Klux Klan. His older brother John recalls the anti-Catholic leaflets periodically left on the porch of the Twomey home.

Lou was 13 years old when Governor Sidney J. Catts campaigned for office brandishing anti-Catholic slogans. When Catts visited Tampa, members of the Sacred Heart parish, where the Twomeys were active members, posted guards around the church buildings as a precaution against possible attack. Lou never forgot what it meant to belong to a minority group. Referring to his own background, he expressed sympathy for rural white Southerners, who felt left out of the economic and civil rights gains enjoyed by the Southern black people to whom he dedicated so much of his energy.

Within the Twomey home religion was central. Timothy Twomey attended Mass every morning and paced the sidewalk in front of the house each evening visibly reciting the rosary. At least once a month priests from Sacred Heart parish came to the Twomeys for dinner. On these occasions the best china, silverware and linens of the prosperous, upper middle-class merchant was tastefully brought out. Mrs. Twomey had been educated at a convent in Philadelphia, Pennsylvania and knew the niceties of hospitality; her husband's expertise in clothing added the right touch of elegance.

On weekends when the Twomey family went to a beach resort, at Pass-a-Grille, then outside St. Petersburg, as much as five hours would be dedicated to ferry and train trips needed to reach a church for Mass. The two sons served as altar boys. A Presbyterian boyhood friend, when learning to serve in his church, was told simply to "observe the Twomey boys" and do the same. Mary, their sister, who dedicated much of her life caring for her parents, was seen going to church as often as two or three times in a single day.

Timothy Twomey's parents had come to America in 1884 during the Irish potato famine. They returned to Ireland later, and Timothy was born there in 1871. In 1875 they returned to America. An older brother, who had been born in this country, provided Timothy with a partnership in a clothing store in Tampa. Their business was successful. The Twomeys were able to change residences three times between 1901 and 1909, the final house being an expansive two-storied structure on South Boulevard in an affluent part of town. The family dressed fastidiously, and in later life Lou Twomey was nearly always impeccably neat, whether in cassock or clerical suit.

Lou attended the Academy of the Holy Names, taught by the Holy Name Sisters, for most of grammar school. During the final years of grammar school and high school he attended Sacred Heart College (the term "college" being used approximately in the French sense of "collège")—now at a new address and known as Jesuit High School. By the time Lou graduated, in June, 1923, the entire student body numbered only 60 and his class only six.

He attained some distinction as a studious boy and was chosen valedictorian. At the same time he was successful in football and baseball. As a catcher he often exploded at the umpire's bad calls. His closest boyhood friend, (now Retired Navy Captain) Ferdinand Fisher, who pitched for the team, recalls the many times he had to calm Lou down. This anger on the ball diamond revealed a side of Lou's character later kept under strict control. "He was one of the most excitable people I've ever known," Captain Fisher recalls. "It always surprised me to see how quickly he blew up and flew off the handle during games. At the same time, his sense of fairness was extraordinary." I asked for an instance of this. "Well," replied Captain Fisher, "once during a football game—he always played half-back—when the opposing team had run out of time-outs, Lou suggested: 'Why don't we let them have one of ours?' I'll never forget that, though I don't remember whether the official allowed it. But I also remember how often he'd blow up, especially during baseball whenever he thought the umpire was wrong. He'd tear off his catcher's mask and yell at the ump. A real Irishman!"

I asked for any other anecdotes from high school days. "There's one that you may find interesting, especially in the light of his later work in behalf of Negroes. We were at a party at someone else's house. Lou picked up a song book from the piano and thumbed through it. When he saw "Marching Through Georgia" he became furious and tore the song out. I've never seen such infinite gall and brass! He was a real died-in-the-wool Southerner."

Lou's older brother, John, recalls a complementary trait: "Louis was never spectacular, just like down the road, methodical and systematic, not spectacular. But he and my father and I used to have all kinds of arguments about everything, sports and everything. But he was never given to self-exploitation. He never cared about publicity. He just did what he thought was right, and that was it."

Lou's social life in high school was rather restricted, but he was popular among his peers. One of them recalls that he was always around to defend the rights of anyone who needed help. Since he was wiry and athletic, his defense had only to be verbal. His facility in rhetoric also came to the fore in formal elocution contests, which Lou consistently won. Despite his successes, friends remember him as exceptionally modest. They also surmised that he was thinking of the priesthood even at that young age.

During his high school years Lou witnessed a major economic calamity among the workers of Tampa. At the end of World War I in 1918 both of the city's major industries, ship building and cigar manufacturing, were in serious difficulty. The Tampa Dock Company and Oscar Daniels Company, which hired a combined work force of over 5,000, ceased operation. Unemployment was serious. In April, 1920, the Cigar Makers Union called a strike in retaliation against the factory owners' attempt to force unions to accept an open shop agreement. A total of 7,613 workers remained on strike for the rest of the year, while 3,500 more employees were thrown out of work. The workers finally had to accept the terms of the owners. This, one supposes, was Lou's introduction to the sort of management-labor problems that would occupy much of his later life.

After graduation Lou attended Georgetown University in Washington, D.C., the oldest Jesuit educational institution in the United States. As a college student he continued the pattern of activities he had followed in high school. Again baseball was his special joy, especially when he hit the winning home run against the Yale team. His classmate and fellow baseball player, Philip McLean, tells of Lou's enthusiasm, too, when he saw his first snowball. "Wouldn't it be great," Lou exclaimed, "if I could only send some snow to my family for them to enjoy?"

McLean recalls Lou's strong loyalty to the Jesuits at Georgetown. It was hardly surprising to anyone who knew him that, even before he completed the course there, he decided that he was called to become a Jesuit. "There wasn't any big celebration in the family when he said he was going to be a Jesuit," his brother remembers. "It didn't surprise anybody, even though he hadn't told us. My father was quite impressed with the Jesuit course of training and how hard it was. When Louis decided to enter, my father said, 'Hope this isn't an instance of trying to put a quart jar in a pint measure.'"

In the fall of 1926 Lou left Georgetown to enter the Jesuit novitiate at Grand Coteau, Louisiana, declining the opportunity to sign a baseball contract with the Washington Senators. The novitiate or noviceship is a two-year period of reflection, prayer and experience during which a young man intending to be a Jesuit attempts to reach a decision. In 1926 the novitiate was a time of almost total seclusion "from the outside world." To the casual visitor it must have appeared something of a cross between monastery and military "boot camp." The daily order was minutely regulated, from the bell for rising at 5:00 to the signal for retiring somewhat after 9:00 in the evening. Meantime almost every minute was scheduled, with stress on prayer, meditation, spiritual reading, manual labor, formal recreation (sometimes called "organized joy"), religious conferences and a rather restricted time for class and study. Today's program, following the developments of Vatican Council II, is so much more flexible and "open" that younger Jesuits find it impossible to imagine the novitiate gone through by their elders.

Different as the modern novitiate style is from the one experienced by Lou Twomey, the core elements remain alike. Plenty of reflection, various forms of prayer (today with more stress on liturgical and communal prayer, with occasional forays into the charismatic or pentecostal modes), discernment with a spiritual director, and most central of all the month-long experience of the Ignatian *Spiritual Exercises.*

Libraries have been written on the subject, and anyone interested in grasping the ultimate motivations of Lou Twomey's life would do well to review Karl Rahner's volume *Spiritual Exercises* or some other recent study, such as Avery Dulles' essay, *The Ignatian Experience As Reflected in the Spiritual Theology of Karl Rahner.* The Ignatian *Exercises* are hard to describe briefly, being a sort of blueprint of key reflections and prayers designed to help the Christian discern God's will and change his life toward one of loving service. Rahner points out that it is only in the experience of affective prayer joined to intellectual endeavor that a person enters into proper union with God. "Neither God nor his self-communication can be adequately represented in conceptual thought and statements," Dulles shows. It is rather through intimate identification with Christ and his life, death and resurrection that one finds the Ignatian ideal. Meditations like "The Kingship of Christ," "The Two Standards" and other vivid symbols of crucial elements of the spiritual life were surely adapted to the growth of as ardent, intense and single-minded a person as Lou Twomey. One surmises that the *Spiritual Exercises* provided precisely the sort of focus required in so energetic and spiritual a person as young Lou seems to have been. His spiritual notes taken during that time suggest as much.

We have no way of knowing what spiritual trials Lou may have faced during his novitiate. His peers remember him with warmth, stressing adjectives like "enthusiastic," "intense," "determined," "competitive," "generous," in their descriptions of his temperament. They repeatedly recall his athletic success during seminary days, as during those of high school and college, and the zest shown in games as well as discussion. My earliest memory of Lou had to do with his legendary athletic prowess and out-going personality.

With allowances made for oversimplification, we find in a letter to a Methodist minister and personal friend what may be a key to his psychic and spiritual structure: "I have never known, nor, please God, will ever know except vicariously what it means to have my inmost being racked by the fearful doubt as to whether or not I possess the Truth. From my earliest years the priceless gift of Absolute Truth, as we Catholics conceive our Faith, has been mine." This sounds authentically pre-Vatican-II. But he goes on less triumphalistically: "But little credit is due me on this account, for had I been left to quest for Truth in my maturer years I might now be numbered among those who failed or even among those who never tried. It is, therefore, with deep and abiding gratitude that I daily thank God for having spared me a struggle from which I might never have emerged." Written a decade after the novitiate, this letter suggests that for Lou this must have been a time of spiritual intensification and enlightenment rather than of crisis.

In charge of the spiritual program at Grand Coteau at this time was Father John Salter, S.J., who would later be provincial, or head, of all Jesuits working in the South. John Salter, who had made something of a record for excellence during his theological studies at Woodstock College, Maryland, was exceptional, too, in his southern pedigree. He was, in fact, grandnephew of Alexander Hamilton Stephens, vice-president of the Confederacy. (I was present, though Lou had already left Grand Coteau, in 1933 when Father Salter was buried next to his brother Jesuit, Father Thomas Ewing Sherman, son of General William Tecumseh Sherman. Sherman died April 29 and Salter May 2. The striking Blue-and-Gray coincidence was not lost on us nor on thousands of subsequent visitors.)

A classmate of Lou Twomey's, E. Cecil Lang, S.J., later provincial of Southern Jesuits, writes warmly of Lou and of Father Salter: "Salter was brilliant, holy, etc., etc. I could go on and on, and among his virtues was a deep, intense love for the Society of Jesus. He was, I think, remarkably successful in passing this love and understanding of the vision of Ignatius to his novices. Lou caught this love and devotion to the Church and to the Society from John Salter."

A difficult decision, however, faced Lou at the end of his first year of novitiate. His brother describes what happened: "My father had a nervous breakdown and Louis came home to help him in the store. My father was in such a condition that he was not making firm decisions. It was evident that Lou wanted to go back to Grand Coteau, but my father wouldn't let him go because he didn't have any self-confidence. After Lou had been back a year or so, I went to my father and told him he had to let Louis go back, because he couldn't stay here forever. If I hadn't done that, I don't know when Louis would have gone back. Father couldn't make up his mind. Yet, he was happy that Louis was to be a priest. So Louis went back. I remember telling somebody that after Louis had taken that period off and gone back, I was very much consoled because I was satisfied then that he really meant it."

When Lou returned to the novitiate in Grand Coteau, in 1929, he was required to start the two-year program over. This was simply a matter of church canon law. At this time, however, there was a new director of novices. On June 26, 1928, the previous director, Father John Salter, was made provincial superior of all the Southern Jesuits. For a matter of months he was succeeded at Grand Coteau by Father Peter Weckx, as acting novice master, until the arrival of Father Thomas Carey, who was in charge at the time of Lou's return.

At the end of his first year, Lou was allowed to do more study than was then customary in novitiates. Since he had already done most of his college work, this second year counted as the equivalent of the two years of "juniorate" studies normally required of young Jesuits at that time. The "juniorate" put considerable stress on linguistic and rhetorical development, with many hours per week of Latin, English, Greek and speech. The transcript of Lou's credits show that he studied two speeches of Cicero in Latin, two of Demosthenes in Greek, plus other Latin, Greek and English authors, together with some European history and pedagogical methods. Since St. Charles College is incorporated into Loyola University, New Orleans, Lou received his bachelor of arts degree from Loyola (on June 8, 1931, not in 1932, as Lou mistakenly wrote in a biographical sketch for his second master's thesis in 1947).

While Lou's linguistic gifts were quite modest, his bent for rhetoric and debate made this year quite congenial. It was not altogether surprising, then, when Anne Marie Richard visited Loyola University in 1970 to interview several of Lou's friends regarding his rhetorical skills. Her study was accepted as a master's thesis at Louisiana State University and brandishes the title "A Rhetorical Analysis of the June, 1958, Radio Speeches of Louis J. Twomey." It is easy to imagine Lou chuckling at the thought of his rhetorical skills being submitted to scholarly analysis.

Lou was approved by his spiritual mentors and allowed to make his vowed commitment to God within the Society of Jesus. The simple ceremony took place before the Grand Coteau Jesuit community during Mass on February 2, 1931. In addition to the traditional vows of poverty, celibacy and obedience, the young Jesuit makes a further promise of entering more definitively into the Society of Jesus in what are known as "final vows." This later ceremony, done with more solemnity and more publicly, takes place some dozen years later and (in the case of Jesuit priests) after ordination. The first vows end with a prayer that God will accept this full offering and give help and grace that the promises be kept. To a person of Lou's enthusiastic temperament the event must have been one of exceptional excitement.

The next step (following novitiate and juniorate) in the Jesuit course of studies common in Lou Twomey's day involved a rather thorough introduction to philosophy—the term understood in the scholastic, more or less neo-Thomistic sense. At that time Southern Jesuits, having no "philosophate" of their own, commonly went to the nearest such institution; that connected with St. Louis University. There Lou renewed and deepened his acquaintance with the scholastic approach to philosophy, going beyond the introduction he had undergone at Georgetown University.

The stress in seminary philosophical training at that time, at least at St. Louis, was severely rational and what is often called essentialist. True, a current of neo-Thomistic existentialism was vital, largely thanks to an inspiring young teacher, Henri Renard, S.J., who expounded on texts of Thomas Aquinas and started a vital movement at least among the more talented students. But, in general, exposure to great scholastic thinkers (Aquinas, Scotus, Suarez and others) was largely at second or third hand. The textbook manual, syllogistic and geared to ready answers, was thought of as something of an ideal. I recall, for example, that full editions of the great masters were available in the library, but a student could spend three years "doing philosophy" without ever having to consult them directly.

This discipline was not without advantages. It promoted habits of thinking that were clear and precise (some would say Cartesian rather than Thomistic), with all doubts or obscurities neatly dispatched through distinctions and sub-distinctions. The course was not altogether dissimilar to that of rhetoric, with precise categories and what an associate called "irrefutability if not conviction." It was strong in formal logic.

In psychology courses stress was placed on freedom of the human will, in ethics on natural law and its consequences. Freedom suggested the possibility of choice and growth, unconditioned by environment or other pressures. Natural law showed man's communitarian nature and the inner structure of personal and social reality available to man by rational probing. In the light of Lou Twomey's subsequent work, it is not hard to perceive in these other scholastic viewpoints a substratum of thinking he must have found sympathetic. Theology, especially moral theology, would go further, providing more explicitly Christian grounding, while not denying human rationality.

In 1933 Lou Twomey completed the philosophy course and was awarded a master of arts degree, following his thesis on the place of hope in the writing of St. Thomas More (who would, in fact, be canonized two years later). The 71-page thesis is of no special distinction, save for its higher than ordinary literacy. Lou contrasts the "decidedly pessimistic attitude of such masters of the written word as Shelley, Lord Byron, and Thomas Hardy" with "the inspiration of More's buoyant optimism." Something of Lou's feeling for heroes comes through. I find this sentence almost autobiographical: "Through his supernatural convictions and aspirations he kept his heart simple, steadfast, undefiled, undeceived in prosperity, undismayed in adversity." More, of course, has since been declared the patron saint of lawyers, and it seems appropriate that from 1947 to 1962 Lou was to be involved in Loyola's Law School as regent and instructor in the philosophy of law.

It is common to interrupt the Jesuit course of studies before the formal study of theology to allow the young seminarian some time of personal creative activity. Normally this is a period of teaching, which serves the double purpose of a break from being on the "receiving end" of studies and service to one or other school under Jesuit direction. An energetic person like Lou Twomey must have been particularly eager to do for others, after what seemed years of academic pursuits.

More often than otherwise, the young "regent" (as the teaching seminarian is called) is sent to a high school. In Lou's case, however, perhaps because of his master's degree and slighty older age, the assignment was to Spring Hill College, in the suburbs (at that time) of Mobile, Alabama. As the oldest Catholic college of Jesuits in the South (indeed of the whole south) and third oldest of Jesuit colleges in the United States, Spring Hill evokes a sense of history and nostalgia. Situated bucolically on a variegated campus of immense size, it attracts students from all over the the country and some foreign countries as well.

Lou was assigned to teach English and Latin, to take charge of the Portier Debating Society, and to serve as prefect of the students, living in the dormitory building with them. Teaching English and debating must have been congenial. His dean at the time, Father Andrew C. Smith, assured me that "he managed good classes in English and Latin and was uncomplainingly faithful to the odious duties of 'prefect.' The boys called him 'The Hound of Heaven'—a good-natured tribute to his perseverance in working with them and al the spiritual good he did them."

A fellow regent remembers how hard Lou worked with his classes, and an apprentice writer, grateful after many years, has this to say: "He spent hours with me going over every line, every word, polishing style, cutting out irrelevancies and useless repetitions, insisting on no split infinitives and no sentences ending in prepositions. He himself was extremely meticulous in his use of English—a purist, many would say." At the same time, as those of us who followed the *Blueprint* recall, and as a friendly critic writes, "he seemed unable to write a sharp, short paragraph; his long and wordy sentences were reminiscent of Archbishop Rummel's pastoral letters."

A contemporary recalls that Lou was very energetic in revitalizing the Portier Debating Society. It is an interesting coincidence that his friend and later associate, Joseph H. Fichter, inherited the debating society from Lou, and turned it over, in 1938, to Albert S. Foley, who was later to do such important social work at Spring Hill College.

Following his three-year teaching experience at Spring Hill College, Lou was sent on to theological studies at St. Mary's College, St. Marys, Kansas. Situated at the edge of a rural Kansas village, St. Mary's College had once been an Indian mission, then a boarding school for boys once rather well known in stories written by Father Francis J. Finn, S.J. The College had closed in the 1930's and became the location of the faculty of divinity of St. Louis University. Rusticated as this faculty was, it included a number of theological scholars of at least national stature. Among them one remembers Gerald Ellard, an internationally respected liturgist; his brother Augustine Ellard, ascetical theologian and later a founder of *Review for Religious* together with the canonist Adam Ellis and the moral theologian Gerald Kelly; the scripture scholar Michael Gruenthaner, later to be editor of the *Catholic Biblical Quarterly;* the archaeologist Augustine Wand; the author of works on comparative religion, George Ring; and several teachers of some distinction as lecturers but not known for publication. The St. Mary's library, including the accumulation of many decades at St. Louis University, was then reckoned one of the two or three finest in American Catholic institutions. Rusic though it was, St. Mary's could not fairly be called the theological boondocks.

Unfortunately for a biographer, Lou Twomey seems to have left us little of his personal reactions to life at St. Mary's and the theological course of studies there. One may reasonably imagine him somewhat restive at the thought of not being able to work directly for others; activist types have always been so during years of academic work, much of which must seem abstract and not evidently relevant. Yet, the time available for prayer and reflection would have been welcome to so spiritual a person as Lou. So would the broad subject matter of theology: the clarification of the experience of God within the Christian heritage. For Lou was, from childhood, thoroughly dedicated to the Church.

Moral theology would have been particularly sympathetic to him, being more obviously practical. Father Francis J. O'Boyle was held in awe among the theological students of that time for his experience and strong pastoral bent. Gerald Kelly, then a young professor and later to become internationally famous, quickly won the respect of students for his down-to-earth approach to moral problems. In later life Lou often complained that social justice was not given the stress needed, at least in formal classes. Yet, considerable ferment was noted at St. Mary's, at least among some students, regarding social problems. (This will be apparent a few paragraphs later). The eminent liturgist Gerald Ellard, S.J., was already stressing social implications of Christian corporate worship and published a brochure in 1938 titled *The Mystical Body and Social Action*. Lou was very much influenced by Ellard and the liturgical movement some time before the papal encyclicals on the subject appeared. I cannot find evidence, however, that much class time was given to the great social encyclicals *Quadragesimo Anno* and *Rerum Novarum*, though during those years papal documents were strongly stressed as theological sources.

These two papal documents became in fact something of a *magna charta* of Lou's social thinking and teaching, a general plan for implementing the ideals and concerns of the Catholic Church for the good of society. Again and again Lou turned to them for inspiration in arguing the case for social justice. When a critic argued that these documents were too vague, Lou replied: "The point I was striving to make . . . is that Catholics do have in official papal pronouncements a set of guidelines to direct them in their thinking and in their acting relative to practical problems. To reject these guidelines is, in my opinion, a very rash thing to do. For they are thought out very carefully in the light not only of Catholic theological teaching but also in the light of developing phenomena in the existential world. These problems do have their theological and moral implications."

While at St. Mary's Lou found time to break into publication. The *Catholic Periodical Index* for 1939-1940 lists three of his articles, which I have enjoyed perusing. "Christ the Workingman" appeared in the June, 1939, issue of the *Catholic World*. In it Lou makes a great deal of the papal encyclicals and of the famed Oswald von Nell-Breuning, leading social thinker of the period. Typical of Lou's thinking is the sentence: "Labor was raised to a noble rank by a divine acolade from the hand of Christ the Workingman." The magazine's editor, identifying the author, has this to say: "One of those responsible for our good opinion of the social consciousness of St. Mary's Kansas is Louis J. Twomey, S.J., champion of the rights and dignity of labor. Mr. Twomey will be ordained this month."

Two other articles published by Lou during theological studies had to do with aspects of liturgy. "To Abstain from Flesh-Meat" appeared in the *Ecclesiastical Review* for February, 1939, and while it is largely the result of research into canon law, we find Lou already talking of the Mystical Body—a relatively new emphasis in those days and rich with social implications. The other, in the May, 1940, issue of the same journal, treats of "The Eucharist Fast," which Lou interprets not so much juridically but as "a vital force in conditioning the soul as well as the body" for the union with Christ. Another article, I am informed by a classmate, was not allowed to be published, since it dealt with several "radical" liturgical notions (later part of Church teaching) like the desirability of consecrating the same bread that would be used at communion in that particular Mass. He was obviously influenced in his liturgical thinking by the pioneer Gerard Ellard.

Busy as he was, Lou found time for others. A classmate told me that when he was struggling over his master's thesis, Lou insisted: "Come on, Joe, let me type it for you." Lou insisted and did the task. (Thirty years later, when Lou was at the peak of his activity and already an international celebrity, he made an even more sacrificial offer. A young teacher at Loyola was afraid that an impending operation might require him to drop classes. Quite simply and undramatically Lou said: "Don't worry. Let me take your classes for you.")

The same classmate added that his first memory of Lou was during an athletic contest when they had almost come to blows. "Lou was always intense in everything he did," he added, "especially when it came to helping people." He went on to reminisce about days when they both taught at Spring Hill. With a flair for writing, Lou was a perfectionist as an English teacher, spending endless hours agonizing over freshman compositions in the struggle to teach youngsters how to write a decent sentence. He was no less demanding on himself.

Ordination, the goal of many years of preparation, came on June 21, 1939. Unfortunately we have no diary or letters to document what must have been the high point of his life. The priesthood, in his eyes, always kept both a transcendental and a horizontal dimension. His dedication to human values was never in competition with an intense and traditional spiritual life. Rather, the latter was the undeviating motivation of his social involvement. In personal letters Lou rarely used formulas. An exception, which we find more or less verbatim in letters to several young persons about to be ordained, seems autobiographical: "Be true to the ideals of the First Priests. Be always another Christ to all men, but especially to the 'little people' wherever you may find them."

A conferee, recalling the enthusiasm with which he looked forward to celebrating Mass, adds this piquant detail: "Lou was always tone-deaf, you know. I spent hours and hours trying to teach him the priest's chants. We were a total failure." His voice, however, though unmusical was powerful, deep and thoroughly effective in public speaking. He used it to advantage.

During Lou's time and for many years after, following ordination and a fourth year of theological studies, the young Jesuit priest normally went on to a year of "second novitiate" or "tertianship" (so called because it was a sort of third year of novitiate). Today it is more common to allow some years of active apostolate between theology and tertianship.

For this year of spiritual concentration Lou was sent to St. Stanislaus Seminary, Cleveland, Ohio (September 1940 to July, 1941). His spiritual director was Francis X. McMenamey, under whom he repeated the Spiritual Exercises of St. Ignatius. I was privileged to read the notes he took then, finding them (in retrospect) very paradigmatic of Lou's future life and work as a priest. The spirituality expressed is thoroughly traditional and would not interest publishers today. One resolution I read with no little poignancy: "sacrifice on smoking again." In view of the fact that Lou later became a chain-smoker and that this caused or aggravated the fatal emphysema of his last years, this unkept decision seems particularly ironical.

Diaries kept during other annual retreats seem more typical. Back in 1938, during a retreat at Spring Hill, he resolved "to do all I can to help others, at the same time recalling: 'In as much as you did to the least of my brethren you did it to me'." This may be taken as the motto of his life. Later, visiting in Tampa, he wrote in his retreat diary for 1955: "To pursue staunchly unpopular causes, e.g. Labor and Race relations, when they seem to promote the Kingdom of Christ."

After tertianship Lou entered the most active phase of his life, though it must have seemed a delaying action, given his later work. He was sent to Jesuit High School, Tampa, his old alma mater, to serve as principal. Students who were there at the time use the same adjectives we meet again and again to describe his presence and work: "intense," "energetic," "demanding," "personal." He was said to have been particularly exacting of his own nephew, then a student, in a sort of reverse nepotism, leaning ever backwards in the interest of fairness. One former student, now a widely respected scholar and author, recalls what seems a significant incident: he had been told he would be valedictorian, since the class so elected him; when Lou heard of this he called the student into his office, apologized sympathetically, but stated that he could not allow school policy to be changed and that another student should be valedictorian, since his grades were highest. At the time the disappointed student found this unduly severe, but in retrospect he sees that it was only an instance of Lou's fairness and consistency.

Anthony C. O'Flynn, S.J., now a theology professor in Rhodesia but then a teacher in Tampa, writes certain reminiscences from those days: "Lou was impeccably polite, addressing us younger Jesuits with the formal title of 'Mister'. As a disciplinarian he was perhaps overkind with the boys. 'If I have to err,' he once told me, 'I'd rather do it in their favor.' Yet he was far from weak: on matters of principle or moral questions he had a will of iron. He was an 'easy touch' but always tried to save beggars' self-respect, saying, 'I'm investing in your future.' While he was principal he would sit on the bench during games and often got in arguments with officials or opposing coaches."

He also managed to be involved in student drilling. On one occasion, during drill he was called to the phone. The students continued marching, since no orders had been given to the contrary. After the phone call Lou became absorbed in other work, entirely oblivious of the marching students, who by then had traveled some distance into the city. Another phone call to the absent-minded principal enabled the students to return to school.

In September, 1945, Lou was able to get into study more directly in line with his future work. Rev. Vincent O'Connell, S.M., director of social action in the archdiocese of New Orleans, spoke to Lou's provincial superior, Thomas Shields, S.J., and proposed that Lou be sent to the Institute of Social Studies, affiliated with St. Louis University. At its head was the respected scholar and labor relations expert Leo Brown, S.J., who took a special interest in Lou's study and directed his thesis.

Father Brown remembers those years vividly. "Lou was unforgettable," he chuckled. "His name still comes up frequently in conversation. It seems that no one who ever met Lou Twomey ever forgot him." I asked Brown to compare Twomey and Daniel Lord, who had headed the Institute of Social Order in St. Louis. "They were alike in their dynamism, enthusiasm, energy. But Dan was no organizer. Lou was. He did more than generate enthusiasm."

"Any interesting anecdotes about Lou?" I asked. "Lots," Father Brown replied. "Let's see. Once at a big affair, Msgr. George Higgins was principal speaker and Lou made the introduction. Lou waxed eloquent, as usual, stressing all George's accomplishments leading up to the introduction: 'And I have the honor to present to you Msgr. John Cronin.' John Cronin was present and roared with pleasure. George acknowledged the exuberant introduction, remarking: 'Lou, you're at your best tonight!' Some of Lou's phrases are still recalled, like 'the Trojan *snake* of communism'; we could never be sure whether it was a slip or whether Lou intended it."

During Lou's years at the Institute of Social Studies he became closely associated with other men whom he would work with later when he became editor of *Social Order* magazine. While this episode —1962-1963—comes somewhat later in his life, it seems appropriate to mention it here in conjunction with Leo Brown.

"How was Lou chosen to be editor of *Social Order?*" I asked. "I can't recall exactly. It seems it was because he could do the job, with his experience in handling the *Blueprint*. Lou had lots of capable friends. He would get them to write the articles. The real editing work was done by Father Herbert Walker, S.J. They made a good team. You should talk to him."

I did and asked Father Walker for his memories about working with Lou. "He was easy to work with, with his endless enthusiasm. It took a lot of humility for him to accept the job, but he did. I was amazed at how many people Lou knew. When he felt an article was needed, he would call the right person and get him to write the article *gratis*. We had so little money to work with. And don't forget the constant flow of Lou's article to *Queen's Work*. I worked with him in the Summer School of Catholic Action. He was tremendously popular and effective. People affectionately called him "God's

Madman." "Why?" I inquired. "Because he was like St. Philip Neri, a fool for Christ. Besides, in the eyes of the uncommitted Lou seemed to have a touch of madness."

Lou had to do a thesis in order to receive the master's degree which he felt he needed for future work. Leo Brown suggested a topic that would be manageable and which he felt Lou might find not altogether uncongenial: "NIRA: An American Pattern for Vocational Organization." This was a study of Franklin D. Roosevelt's National Industrial Recovery Act of May, 1933. Like most M.A. theses, it is hardly of earth-shaking importance. Yet, to one interested in Lou's life, reading it proved of some interest.

His Introduction is a fair sample of the rhetoric associated with Lou's later writing. It opens (unsurprisingly) with a quotation from Pope Leo XIII: " 'The momentous seriousness of the present state of things just now fills every mind with painful apprehension.' Although written by Leo XIII on May 15, 1891, as a commentary on the crisis of his own day, these words with even greater force reflect the mentality of thinking men of this day. World War II is over; at least organized fighting on defined battlefronts is done. And yet 'painful apprehension' of a third and more terrible world war grows daily more intense as the diplomats of the United Nations argue and counter-argue themselves into sickening frustration. The inevitable effects of this international impasse are making themselves felt within our own borders so that the home front presents problems of explosive possibilities."

Aside from the urgency omnipresent in Lou's writings and speeches, there appear in the thesis certain of his favorite themes: e.g., the failure of "our American educational system in developing social consciousness among its students"; "even Catholic education has in large measure concentrated on training its subjects to be good individuals . . . but in preparing its students to fulfill their obligations as members of society, it has been seriously delinquent." He then quotes Pius XI and his insistence on "an intensive program of social education." Even worse, "our seminaries have given slight heed to the equally solemn directive of the same Pope: 'all candidates for the sacred priesthood must be adequately prepared . . . by intense study of social matters'." Later Lou would never lose an opportunity to deplore the lack of social awareness provided by the seminary course he had gone through.

During these years with the Institute of Social Sciences Lou returned to publication, with an article in *Today's World* (May, 1946), to be reprinted in the *Catholic Digest* (January, 1947). It deals with another of his favorite themes: the need of cooperation rather than mere confrontation. The following excerpt is altogether typical of Lou's approach: "Interpreting labor history with his sympathy rather than his judgment, an open-minded person can scarcely resist becoming an avowed, and prejudiced, champion of labor. To emphasize the injustice suffered by labor may help get the picture into proper perspective and incite sincere repentance in management, but when such emphasis is used to stir up enmity and encourage revenge, it is as dangerous as it is un-Christian."

I asked Leo Brown, his mentor during these years, to recapitulate his memory of Lou. This was his reply: "A great man, passionately devoted to justice—not justice in the abstract, but justice for people. Whenever he saw someone suffering from injustice he was strongly moved to do something about it. Even back in the stormy forties, when St. Louis University was being integrated, Lou, though still a student, was very outspoken. Even then he was 'colorblind.' But what was most remarkable about him was the fact that he went out and did things. Lou was no genius, of course. But he never let worries about his own limitations or his lack of special capacities get in the way. He did things and did them very well."

Following this period of social studies Lou felt fired to start what would be his life's work. He went to Loyola University, New Orleans, to join the faculty and set up his Institute of Industrial Relations.

Chapter 3
LABOR

"America's most interesting city. That is how very many people refer to New Orleans. And there is much to support the reference. New Orleans is and always has been a major seaport; it is now the second largest in the United States. It is also a river town situated on one of the world's most fabulous waterways. 'Old Man River' has contributed generously of its own majesty and romanticism to help shape the character of New Orleans.

"Perhaps in no other city of the Northern hemisphere does the old blend with the new as charmingly as in New Orleans. One part is centuries old; the other as new as the morning newspaper. The quaint narrow streets of the French Quarter are in striking contrast to the magnificent boulevards of the modern city."

This sounds very much like a chauvinistic, Chamber of Commerce brochure enticing visitors to the Crescent City, promoting its second industry, tourism. It is, rather, the opening of a radio speech, delivered by Lou Twomey, June 29, 1958, as part of a series on race for the "Christian in Action" program broadcast on ABC. Like any effective orator, Lou starts in a way calculated (as the rhetoricians say) to make listeners "benevolent," at least his New Orleans listeners. For though his audience was nation-wide, his podium was, and had been since 1947, New Orleans.

A previous chapter told of the modest beginnings of Lou's principal institutional creation—the Institute of Industrial Relations (later known as the Institute of Human Relations). While budget and facilities were miniscule, Loyola University provided a base of operations and a faculty position which offered academic status. As previously mentioned, Lou, in fact, always made use of his position. The printed page of biographical data which he regularly provided started with the words "Father Twomey is a member of the faculty of Loyola University of the South at New Orleans, Louisiana. He has served as the Regent of the Law School at Loyola University and has taught the philosophy of law. He is the Director of the Institute of

Father Twomey, Director of the Institute of Human Relations

Human Relations of Loyola University, formerly known as the Institute of Industrial Relations, which he founded in October of 1947."

The catalogue listing activities of Jesuits in the South for 1947-1948 describes him as "Director of the Institute of Industrial Relations" but immediately adds "Lecturer in Philosophy." The following year's catalogue changes the order, putting in first place "Regent of the School of Law." The term "Regent," which he used until the end of the school year of 1962, meant, in the context of a number of Jesuit colleges and universities, a Jesuit who was not dean but who cooperated with the dean, serving as a link between the college and the Jesuit community. It was a prestige title, and while Lou Twomey was totally unconcerned about pomp and circumstance, he doubtless saw that it would add weight ("clout" we would say today) to his statements and endeavors for social causes.

"Lecturer in Philosophy" meant concretely lecturer in jurisprudence or the philosophy of law. A faculty member of the Law School recalls how harmoniously Lou worked with his colleagues and how effective he was. in helping the Law faculty integrate the school two years before the Brown Decision. Despite considerable opposition from alumni, in 1952 the Law School admitted its first black students: Ben Johnson and Norman Francis (today the first lay president of Xavier University in New Orleans). But his on-going work as lecturer involved changing racial and other social attitudes among aspiring lawyers. His effectiveness in this could be easily documented from letters sent him by former students and tributes after his death.

When he left his assignment in Tampa to do graduate work in St. Louis, Lou had already projected a school at Loyola to serve the need for education in family relations, industrial relations, interracial justice and rural life. (Indeed, he had requested permission from the superior of Jesuits in the South, Thomas J. Shields, to open a labor school. We have Lou's letter of April 7, 1940, and the response dated April 13, was that he should go immediately to tertianship.)

It was Father Shields' successor as superior of Southern Jesuits, Harry L. Crane, who gave the mandate for the new institute. Crane circulated a letter to all Jesuit communities in the South informing them of the new endeavor under Lou's direction. He pointed out that the supreme Jesuit legislative body, the General Congregation of 1939, had directed each region or province of Jesuits to begin concrete programs for implementing the goals of social reform articulated in the popes' social encyclicals. Social institutes were explicitly listed among such programs. Crane also made careful mention of a problem acutely facing Southerners: justice for racial minorities.

When Twomey arrived in New Orleans to begin a non-accredited institute, there seemed nothing about him to upset even the most reluctant supporters of social justice. He spoke without rancor and, as always, dressed with clerical propriety. The local press acknowledged his arrival and quoted a statement given by Lou: "Representatives of labor and management will be kept together in the courses purposely so they may study and learn together." The *Maroon*, Loyola's school paper, ran a front page story on the Institute and displayed a picture of the youthful priest whose features seemed to exhibit both determination and an affable personality.

The effort at reconciliation that marked Twomey throughout his public career was apparent from one of his first statements about the Institute. "It is dedicated to building the spirit of cooperation between management and labor. It is not pro-management; it is not pro-labor; it is not subsidized by either group. It is a public service of the University. Its purpose is to afford a common ground upon which management and labor can work together in mutual helpfulness toward the solution of their mutual problems." He went on to stress: "Management cannot do without labor, nor labor without management. Both perform essential functions in society. . . . They are interdependent units of the same organic whole; therefore, what is good for one is good for the other, and what hurts one hurts the other."

This theme, which may strike some as platitudinous and others as naive, ran like a *leitmotiv* through lecture after lecture, article after article. We find Lou constantly reiterating such ideals, pleading with both management and labor to "quit their class struggle, their charges and counter-charges, their mutual distrust and suspicion." In anyone less intense or transparently honest the pleas would have seemed outrageously idealistic. Yet great numbers of people took him seriously. Motivation he offered "in the spirit of Christian and democratic loyalty to American ideals." More pragmatically he insisted that only such a magnanimous spirit could enable New Orleans to realize the "vast industrial possibilities" of the area. The success of such enterprises depended, he stated, "on men of management and men of labor who attack the problems of industrial relations not with the narrow view of selfish gain and special privilege." Rather their vision had to be that of "high-principled leaders sincerely and courageously dedicated to the application of justice, good faith and fair dealing."

Lou was attempting then what more recently has been called "consciousness-raising." In a brochure announcing courses for 1947, he italicized a famous quotation from St. Augustine: "In essential things, unity; in non-essential things, liberty; in all things, charity." Four courses were offered: one in general theory ("Industrial Ethics"), one in information ("Current Industrial Problems"), and two in basic skills necessary for participation in union organization ("Public Speaking and Parliamentary Procedure" and "Principles and Practices of Collective Bargaining").

Since his monthly budget was only twenty dollars, Lou had no way of paying instructors. He secured the voluntary help of an instructor in Loyola's Business School, Ivor Trapolin, who was to remain a close friend and associate. Trapolin tells a humorous anecdote of that first year. He and Twomey were working on urgent matters; a cleaning lady knocked on the door and asked to speak with Father Twomey on some personal problem. Trapolin left the small office and paced the corridor outside for more than an hour. When the janitress left, Trapolin reminded Lou that they were behind in meeting a deadline. Lou replied quite unaffectedly: "Ivor, before anything, any job, I am a priest." That, concluded Trapolin in an interview, "was the story of his life."

It can hardly be proven, but it is equally hard to doubt, that the growth of Lou's venture was not due simply to its intrinsic merit. As one reads speech after speech, article after article by Lou Twomey, one gets a feeling that everything seems so obvious as hardly to be worth saying. At the same time, his idealism in expecting the cooperation of normally opposed interests seems more stratospheric than down to earth. Those who knew Lou have no problem, however, in grasping how he repeatedly accomplished the impossible. The overworked term charisma is perhaps most apposite here; there was something about Lou's transparency, his intense sincerity, his palpable unselfishness, his endless but exhausting drive, that made him hard for the open-minded to resist.

So it was that by the second semester of the Institute's operation more staff members from the faculty of Loyola and from professional circles within New Orleans were attracted to offer courses. His staff already included Father Jacques Yenni, S. J. (with a doctorate in economics); Paul Barker, chief law officer for the National Labor Relations Board in New Orleans; Carl Buchmann, attorney; John Schwab, vice-president of a prominent business firm; and Francis Kennedy, professor in the Loyola School of Business Administration.

While Lou continued to attract management and labor representatives under one roof to reason together, the Institute soon became more labor-oriented. Very likely management found the idealism and efforts to teach basic skills of less immediate self-interest, and in the course of years fewer business firms sent personnel to attend courses.

This troubled Twomey, since he never ceased hoping to bring about constructive meetings between the two sectors. But management always found him too pro-labor. This, as Fichter remarks, "turned off business firms."

Lou's belief in the power of the printed word led him to launch the bulletin called Christ's *Blueprint for the South* (as was mentioned in a previous chapter). This started in 1948, and though I believe it was to be his farthest reaching forum, the work was not officially mentioned in the Southern Jesuit catalogue until the 1955-1956 issue. Perhaps even Lou did not dream of its future impact.

At the same time, he knew clearly what he was about. In the third issue of the *Blueprint,* to the question as to what his and other institutes were doing he replied unequivocally: "They are trying to do just what St. Ignatius tried to do and what the Society (of Jesus) has been trying to do ever since: to evaluate the force of the groundswells in civilization, and to direct that force towards Christ. Our opportunity in the South is particularly promising. Two great changes are taking place in our culture: industrialization and a readjustment of racial relations."

A Jesuit reflecting on this statement and variants of it in some 200 issues of the *Blueprint* notes the effective rhetoric employed. An appeal is made to Jesuit *esprit de corps*—a trait seldom notably absent from Jesuits of Lou's generation; this includes an appeal to the vision of St. Ignatius and a somewhat idealized précis of Jesuit involvement in the task of converting civilization to Christ. The implicit, and ineluctable, conclusion calls for support from other Jesuits. Nor did the appeal to Southern culture and opportunity damage his case. One senses here, as just about everywhere in his speeches and writings, the tactics of a man who might be interiorly as simple as a dove but was rhetorically gifted with the shrewdness of the proverbial serpent.

His approach to people who were not brother Jesuits was equally strategic. To them he would appeal on the basis of American fair play and a sense of justice. Back in 1941, when addressing a meeting of the Tampa Business and Professional Woman's Club, he cited the Declaration of Independence, the Constitution, and the Bill of Rights: "With these documents America is today, and please God, will ever remain, a nation in which even the lowest can proudly boast he is still a free man possessing identical rights with the highest." (Note the use of "he" and "man" in an address to women in those halcyon preliberation days).

Yet the faith dimension of his own life and his conviction that human dignity rested squarely on the reality of God's existence, impelled him to assert his theism no matter what the circumstances. In the same address to the women of Tampa he insisted that " 'inalienable rights' is just an empty phrase unless there is a God to give them sanction." Further he stated that "upon its acceptance in theory and practice depends our survival as free American people." That this might be challenged by pragmatists or utilitarians did not seem to trouble Lou Twomey.

Again and again he appealed to patriotism as a motive for harmonious management-labor relations. In a speech titled "Let's Sell the American Way of Life," he concluded that both management and labor "must accept this approach in relationships if we are to have peace, greater production, and an invincible America." To the Wholesale Distributors Association of Houston he pleaded, in 1951, for justice and charity in the economic order, contending that America had the basic principles of law to make that dream a reality: "If ever a nation had a rendezvous with destiny, that nation is our own. And it is America's destiny under God to lead the world back to the open road of peace, of justice, of freedom, if America will only prove true to its better self." In the light of what a more jaded generation might dub archaic jingoism, it seems bizarre indeed that Lou could ever have been accused of being un-American or even Communist.

Thematic in his writings and speeches is, of course, the dignity of man as foundation for the social order. Under the heading "Our Objective" in an Institute brochure, *A Sketch: The Institute of Human Relations,* we find the dual motto, printed in italics: "To make the dignity of man the heart of economic efficiency" and "Peace, the Fruit of Justice and Charity." This second phrase was printed on the masthead of the *Blueprint* after Lou's death.

Despite his winningness (many people have described him to me as the most dynamic and persuasive speaker they have ever experienced), Lou often met hostile, sometimes sensationally hostile, responses. During his first summer of touring with the SSCA (1948, as described in a previous chapter), he blames the National Association of Manufacturers for lending their support to opponents of a housing bill before Congress, opposing a tax repeal on the sale of oleomargarine, and their general record of attempting to prevent what he considered wise "social legislation." The president of the N.A.M., Morris Sayre, saw a newspaper report of Lou's address (in the Milwaukee *Journal*). He responded in the same newspaper by calling Father Twomey's thinking "pure socialism" and charging that his "kind of fuzzy thinking was responsible for a lot of the troubles in our country." Lou was never one to avoid a debate, and the fight was on.

The secretary of the Dairy Council of Milwaukee, Charles Dineen, complained to Edward J. O'Donnell, S. J., president of Marquette University: "Father Twomey must be very badly informed on the oleo question. If he was well-informed, he would know that this effort of the millionaire manufacturers of oleo would simply be opening the door to further fraud on the consuming public." Such a development, argued Dineen, would lead to the next move of "these exploiters of the public, making cheese of vegetable oils, while trading, of course, all the time on the good name of dairy products." We have Lou's carefully researched replies and a letter to the president of Marquette. In them he cited reports on the hearings in both the House and Senate and noted that the reports verified that at least ten independent organizations and public advocacy groups favored repeal. He added, somewhat typically: "Let me hasten to add that I'm building no brief for 'the millionaire manufacturers'—my thought in this regard is that we've got too many multi-million dollar corporations in this country as it is."

Sayre's denunciations, which Lou thought "rather flippant," elicited a stronger reaction. To Bruno Bitker, a Milwaukee lawyer who had sent Lou the newspaper account of Sayre's attack, he wrote a letter of thanks, adding that "it does little credit to Mr. Sayre to have recourse to the reactionary label of 'socialism' when thinking not in accord with his out-moded type is expressed." In another letter to Bitker, Lou used an article in the *Harvard Business Review* as an indictment of the National Association of Manufacturers' policies. He found it "something of a real tragedy that so many liberal minded industrialists in the N.A.M. have such little influence in fashioning its policies."

To substantiate the position he had taken and to gather further information about the N.A.M., Lou wrote Senator Joseph C. O'Mahoney of Wyoming requesting a "pertinent set of statistics concerning the concentration of power and control in present-day American industry." Senator O'Mahoney sent a detailed reply regarding the "so-called 'independent' distributors of oil and gas products," which, like the automobile dealers, are " 'independent,' but in name only." While hardly a scholar in the high academic sense, Lou was a person who always took his home-work seriously.

One of the more gratifying results of the publicity given in the Milwaukee press was the friendship begun between Lou and H. L. Nunn of the Nunn-Bush Shoe Company. Nunn wrote that he had seen the newspaper articles: "About the National Association of Manufacturers, I feel exactly as you do." He further stated his reservations about the "question of laissez faire capitalism" and confided to Twomey that while it seemed acceptable in theory, in a "society as complex as ours, it seems a bit too much like the law of the jungle."

The successful career of H. L. Nunn as a businessman, his personal warmth, and the plans he had devised for his own employees to share in the profits of the shoe company provided Twomey with practical advice as well as moral support.

About the time that this friendship began, Nunn was invited to lecture on "Personnel in Industry" at the University of Texas. He wrote Lou that he intended to emphasize the fact that "businessmen, as a rule, look upon labor as a commodity."

Many letters, however, were negative. A. B. Bussman wrote from St. Louis: "I have a considerable file of written articles and talks made by our clergy and even members of our hierarchy all in the same destructive vein as your address, and I can truthfully say to you that I am heartsick to realize that our Catholic young people are being fed such un-Christian doctrine by our clergy." Lou's reply to Bussman was typical. Courageously he declined to reply to mere allegations; instead he appealed to the brotherhood of man in Christ: "There is no doubt in my mind that the vast majority of my fellow priests engaged in the vitally important social apostolate are doing so at the price of tremendous self-sacrifice, making a vast contribution to the spread of Christ's message to a world that has lost its way." The style and tone of his reply made a friend of an antagonist.

Twomey gave another address in St. Louis two years later that also offended Bussman. He informed Lou that he and "a good many other honest Catholic businessmen were greatly disturbed by the utterances and writings of a number of members of the Jesuit Order." He went on to propose a meeting between himself and his business associates and interested clergy. Twomey attended the meeting in St. Louis and later, in a letter to Bussman, acknowledged his satisfaction: "I want you to know that it was a real pleasure to discuss on such open and frank terms the vital issues involved in our economic and social life."

While courteous, Lou always spoke without equivocation and delivered his views forcefully. He defended his manner in a letter to the executive secretary of the Sheet Metal Contractors' National Association: "I know very well that the address I delivered on the occasion of your recent convention in New Orleans concerned itself with controversial matters. I also know well that what I said did not please some in the audience. However, I have long since made up my mind that it served no useful purpose for people to hear only what they wanted to hear." In three separate addresses Twomey gave detailed explanations as to why the bill was objectionable:

"There is no such thing as limited freedom. Freedom remains genuine only to the extent that it is exercised within reasonable limits." Moral law determined those limits, and in the area of economic relationships and in the relationship of employer-employee, the requirements of justice demand that "the wage and other conditions of work be such as to accord with the intrinsic dignity of the human personality." No right-to-work was absolute, Lou argued. "No man or woman, for instance, has a right to a job for which neither training nor experience fits them. If realistic limitations conditioned the freedom of those seeking employment, then employers, too, had legitimate bounds to their conduct. Unions provided protections for the workers without which they could be exploited on the "immoral principle that human labor is a commodity." If agency shop agreements, by which workers sharing in the benefits acquired through collective bargaining of union representatives also shared the burden of maintaining the union organization, were prohibited, then unscrupulous employers might undermine the gains of labor by hiring enough non-union workers to simply dislodge the unions or make them impotent as spokesmen for the employees. Right-to-work laws provided management with an instrument potentially destructive of the labor movement. Furthermore, Twomey saw it as a violation of the constitutional right of free assembly.

Within three days after Twomey spoke before the legislators, Catholics opposed to this position published an anonymous statement in the New Orleans *Times-Picayune*. They denied that Twomey spoke authoritatively as a representative of the Roman Catholic Church and in fidelity to the doctrine contained in the papal social encyclicals. The statement was sponsored by a "Catholic Laymen's Committee." Later another such statement appeared in the Sunday edition of the same paper with the signatures of 66 Catholics from the vicinity.

Twice again Twomey spoke before the legislators, assuring them of his title as spokesman for Archbishop Rummel. With characteristic thoroughness he documented the harmony of the pro-union stand and the teachings of the papal encyclicals. He then constructed the argument defending the right of the hierarchy to speak out on such vital issues. He argued that the right-to-work issue was a harshly debated moral issue and asked: "And to whom should conscientious men, Catholic and non-Catholic, turn in such a need, if not to their religious leaders?" "If a religious leader would refuse, for fear of criticism, of financial reprisal, or for whatever other reason to take the risks always inherent in any type of meaningful leadership, that leader would be guilty of a serious dereliction of duty."

Twomey did not argue that every Catholic had to view the right-to-work laws his way. He defended freedom to disagree, with this qualification: "But when these issues are vested with serious moral implications, it comes with ill grace and misguided independence that Catholics equate their own conclusions with those of their recognized spiritual leader." (Like any debater, Lou was not altogether unselective in quoting authorities. Once, when he thought the Pope in error on a social question, he sadly told a friend: "I wish the Holy Father hadn't said that.")

Despite Lou's forensic prowess, the right-to-work bill became law in Louisiana in 1954. While two years later it was repealed, the setback to the labor movement cost a great deal. Lou had no illusions about why the bill passed, nor about the fact that repeal came with costly compromise. "In my opinion," he wrote William Lee at Catholic University, "there is no doubt that by and large the core of our problem was political. From my observations, all the arguments on an intellectual basis were pretty futile. Both in the passage and in the repeal political pressures were the dominant feature." He recognized, at least in retrospect, that his addresses before the legislators had been merely "for the record." Nevertheless, as he wrote Lee, there were no regrets, and he felt he had gained "the lasting confidence of the entire labor movement in this area, at the cost of serious 'misunderstanding' with large segments of the business community." Furthermore, he acknowledged that "labor had much that is wrong with it, but the right-to-work legislation is not the solution." What he did not specify was that after the bill's repeal there was a charge leveled at the AFL-CIO in the cane state.

As reported by Paul Jacobs in *The Reporter* (November 1, 1956), the law was repealed in consequence of a "deal" with the cane growers and Louisiana Labor Council. The LLC union officials allegedly agreed to abandon the cane workers and their struggling union in the fight for collective bargaining in return for the repeal of the right-to-work laws. Twomey kept this article on file and was not reluctant about chastizing labor for its failure. As usual, however, he offered such criticism only when he felt confident that he was dealing with those who at least understood the legitimate concerns of the workers. In the senate he admitted publicly that labor had no unassailable claims to innocence. And to his friend, James O'Brien, a national officer of the United Steelworkers in 1959, Lou stated: "Sometimes I wonder who, if anyone, is doing the thinking for the Labor Movement. Believe me, Jim, I do not like the looks of things. The disclosure of the McClellan Committee were not damaging enough. On the local level here in New Orleans, we are faced with severe internal dissension among the local unions." He further confessed to O'Brien that he had grown a "little cynical as to their sincerity." This was with regard to union men who acknowledged "that we have in Loyola's Institute of Industrial Relations is just what they need." Verbal approval helped little when financial strain was crushing for Twomey.

Victor Bussie, the present president of the Louisiana AFL-CIO reported to Ray Ariatti, Twomey's close confidant and associate in the Institute, that Lou "minced no words in scolding the labor unions; he corrected us many times; sometimes it was bitter; always it was right." Lou learned much from Bussie, including his best pro-union arguments according to Joseph Fichter).

The more the anti-labor forces realized how strongly Twomey fought for the workers' cause, the more they dismissed him as a radical. He keenly felt that the resentment he experienced was the consequence of misunderstandings. Meantime, he maintained close personal ties with some representatives of management and with those in the academic and legal professions who admired him and respected his aims. One such friend was Harry Charbonnet, who gave generously to the Institute and who tried unsuccessfully to persuade the affluent Catholic Serra Club to donate funds. Lou thanked Charbonnet and added: "I am quite aware that our efforts in this office are not evaluated in their proper light by many Catholics. Maybe it is my fault. But, honestly, it is extremely difficult, as you know, to preach Catholic social doctrine and to work toward its implementation with people who largely, through no fault of their own, really do not know what Catholic social doctrine really means. Of course, I have made mistakes. But what I can't see is that too many Catholics are quick to form definitive adverse judgments relative to the Institute's activity without being willing to give me a fair chance to explain what our purposes are."

This letter, I find, expresses pithily what I often heard Lou say at length. He found it hard to believe that others could be unfair toward his work, judging rather that they must be misguided. Nor could he understand why others were unwilling to debate a position openly. At the same time, he exhibited no personal acrimony toward those aligned against his Institute.

In 1959 President Eisenhower, through Vice-President Nixon, sent him an invitation to participate in a conference sponsored by the President's Committee on Government Contracts. Later he accepted the invitation of Secretary of Labor Willard Wirtz to serve on the

National Manpower Advisory Committee from 1965 to 1967. As a member of that committee, he continued to serve the cause of unionization for workers, while never letting the labor unions forget their abandonment of the cane workers. Testifying before the National Advisory Commission on Rural Poverty in 1967, Lou told the committee members: "Organized labor is seriously lagging in providing apprenticeship and employment opportunities for rural poor, especially for those who are also minority group members."

Despite the objections of some local businessmen, the president of Dominican College in New Orleans, Sister Mary Louise, O. P., invited Walter Reuther to give the 1965 commencement address. She wrote Lou: "If we do succeed in getting Mr. Walter Reuther to give the commencement address it will be because of your assistance." They did succeed.

In the South, and in New Orleans, the only large Catholic center in the South, Lou's challenging approach and relentless energy made conflict inevitable. John Nelson, a personal friend and one of those closest to Twomey in professional endeavors, attended the Law School at Loyola during Lou's early years there. Since all law students were required to attend the Twomey course on natural law, they quickly became associated. During the war Nelson had been wounded and won several medals for bravery, and as an undergraduate he had been president of the student body. Soon Nelson joined the volunteer faculty of the Institute. Their friendship changed the career of the lawyer and provided Twomey with a complementary spokesman in civic circles ordinarily not open to the clergy. In time the Nelson family, Jack, Marie and their four daughters, became a second home for Twomey and a haven in the limited time he allowed himself to rest, especially on Sunday evenings.

As one reviews his appointment books, the schedule of public addresses, the volume of writing, the courses in both Institute and Law School, the prolific correspondence, and recalls his constant availability for personal and spiritual counseling, one is almost aghast. The pace of his life must have required exceptional interior strength. We who knew Lou Twomey know that that strength came through an intense and faithful prayer life. The Nelsons recall that no matter who might be visiting with them, Lou had no reluctance about withdrawing to devote time to the Divine Office (psalms and other prayers that priests are required to say daily). While unostentatious, Lou was never timid about praying even in the presence of others whenever he judged it appropriate.

Jack Nelson sees in Lou's spirituality a key insight into Lou's zealous and crusading character. Early in their friendship Lou told his staff that the issue of labor organization and that of civil rights for the blacks were "two sides of the same coin." He went on: "the test of integrity of a Catholic's religious faith is in his commitment to the cause of human rights."

Accordingly, in 1950, after asking advice from his staff, Lou determined to integrate fully all classes sponsored by the Institute. This was one of the first, if not the first, instance since Reconstruction of integrated education on a college campus in the deep South. The initial reaction might have been explosive, not only for the classes but for the Institute itself. Twomey personally presided and by his clear argument and persuasive eloquence won over any racists present. In 1951, using the pseudonym Charles A. Lynch, he did a series of articles on integration in the *Queen's Work,* which was issued as a pamphlet entitled *How to Think About Race.* (I personally drew on this pamphlet, as well as on the immense pioneer work of John LaFarge, S.J., in preparing two pamphlets a decade later: *Let's Talk Sense About the Negro* and *What Do They Want Now?*)

Lou's involvement in the SSCA meant a trip to Europe, as escort to a group of students on pilgrimage to Rome for the Holy Year of 1950. The occasion offered visits to the slums of Rome. He met representatives of the student-sponsored Conferenza di S. Vincenzo de Paoli that worked for the destitute. On his return to America, Lou solicited support for this group, and a year later a letter from Rome acknowledged gifts of over $1,200 from American friends—a sizable sum in those days. Lou replied gratefully, while urging the young Italians to "acknowledge personally or through a representative every contribution which is sent to you."

Aware of the importance of implanting social attitudes among those most likely to influence others, Lou treated future teachers and other educators with special attention. The immediate forum for his own presentation of views was the Loyola Law School. At that time Jesuits had thirteen out of twenty Catholic law schools in the United States. The social performance of these law schools left much to be desired, in his estimation.

Lou wrote the editor of a private but respected publication called *Woodstock Letters,* printed largely for American Jesuits. He was characteristically direct: "There are too few of us who are willing honestly to ask ourselves a simple question: 'Are we doing the job we think we are doing?'" He suggested a series of articles on Jesuit law schools, recommending that William Kenealy, S. J., dean of the Boston College Law School, write the first. "Kenealy will do a first class constructively critical job." Since these articles would be read only by Jesuits, he urged that they "need pull no punches," since "we (in the law schools) need a good working-over."

Two years previously he had written to another Jesuit at Woodstock College (then in Maryland) about what he felt was the broader failure of Jesuit schools to "turn out socially alert graduates." With the kindness that always went in counterpoint with his relentlessly honest judgments about his fellow Catholics and their limited accomplishments, he wrote: "It is not that they are not sincere, but even in our schools, especially in our business schools, they have been fed largely on the diet of liberalistic economics with the customary emphasis being placed on individualism."

This theme, which repeatedly emerged whenever Twomey gave his assessment of Jesuit and Catholic schooling in general, challenged his fellow educators for their lack of responsibility in teaching the Catholic doctrine of social justice. He never attributed that negligence to malice and felt certain that if he taught enough courses, wrote incessantly and spoke publicly to the point of exhaustion, the need for motivation and information for teachers would be met and improve the consciousness of everyone. Others shared his feeling that Catholic schools did nothing more than secular schools to create concern about social justice. A nun wrote him from Missouri that, while she enjoyed teaching, "most of these senior lads and lassies are veritable pagans in their attitude toward social problems." This was all a number of years before Lou's friend and colleague, Joseph H. Fichter did his revealing research on these problems as treated in Jesuit high schools (dealt with in chapter 6 of *One-Man Research*).

Those Catholics opposed to Twomey never had cause to feel they were not in good company or without claims to orthodoxy. His seriousness led him to worry about what he called the "lethargy which seems to hang like a pall over the vast majority of Catholics and even of Jesuits." He confessed that he had "struggled long with the problem and felt that too many of our own Catholic people are solidly bourgeois, taking sides almost unconsciously with the vested interests, the very interests which, by horrible excesses, have contributed to the crisis threatening freedom and decency everywhere." This degree of bluntness was shown in a private letter, since he felt a degree of loyalty to the Society of Jesus that did not permit that kind of frank criticism in public. To a professor at Catholic University in Washington he wrote that "our work is fascinating if withal little understood by the majority of Catholics who are graduates of our own schools."

In a matter of years following the founding of the Institute

Twomey's name became known to many Catholics concerned with reform, and they often appealed to him for help beyond his capacities. From Oklahoma City came a letter from someone trying to organize workers but who found his parish priest resentful. According to his correspondent, the priest was helped by a wealthy Catholic in all his personal and institutional financial needs. Twomey replied that he could be of little help but also stated his conviction that occasional kindness did not justify an immoral economic policy: "Regardless of what outside charity an employer may give, his primary obligation is to provide his workers with living wages, human conditions, and decent hours of work. If an employer fails in this obligation, no amount of outside charity excuses him."

The range of activities undertaken by Twomey after he founded the Institute encouraged him to seek the aid of another Jesuit as a full-time staff member. Though he constantly drew from the faculty of Loyola, recruited volunteers from Tulane University, Xavier University, and Dominican College on occasion, and depended on the faithful dedication of lawyers like Paul Barker, Ivor Trapolin and John Nelson, he felt the need for another Jesuit to work exclusively in the Institute. Repeatedly he asked the superior of the Southern Jesuits for one. Two Jesuits with full teaching assignments at Loyola who helped him immeasurably were Jacques Yenni, S. J., and Joseph Fichter, S. J. Both men gave Twomey loyal friendship as well as a generous commitment of their time and scholarly resources. But he needed more.

Even while his requests for a permanent Jesuit assistant were being made, Twomey assumed added obligations by participating in and often acting as officer or board member of various humanitarian, ecumenical and Catholic organizations: the National Conference of Christians and Jews, the Urban League, the Southern Regional Council, the Louisiana Credit Union, the Knights of Columbus, the Catholic Committee of the South, the National Catholic Welfare Conference, the National Council of Catholic Men, the Catholic Business Association.

Most significant for Lou's work over a number of years was the CCS (Catholic Committee of the South). This grew out of the National Catholic Social Action Conference, founded in Cleveland in 1939. This was first headed by Rev. Timothy O'Connell, who was succeeded by Lou's great friend and supporter, Rev. Vincent O'Connell, S. M. (no relative of Tim). Since no one had come to the Cleveland meeting from the South this fact was pointed out. The following year, thanks to the initiative of a Richmond, Virginia, layman, Paul D. Williams, the South was thoroughly represented and organized into the Catholic Conference of the South (CCS); since, however, the term "Conference" seemed to some bishops to suggest a sort of rival, separatist group, the "C" was changed into "Committee."

The CCS established a ten-point goal, pressing for social reform, a just return for human labor, better understanding between capital and labor, a Christian understanding among Southerners irrespective of race or creed. The group met frequently in various Southern cities until its demise in 1956. According to Joseph Fichter, its vitality was very much due to Vincent O'Connell. "It was practically dead by 1950," Fichter reports, "and only the interracial sub-committee—the Commission on Human Rights—remained alive, and that only in New Orleans."

The Southern Regional Council, too, was a favorite activity of Lou Twomey in efforts to campaign for human rights in the South. The archbishop of New Orleans, Joseph Francis Rummell, was strong in backing the same causes. The Council, with an exemplary record of research and reform for social justice, gradually gained national recognition. A study for Columbia Broadcasting System reported that, from 1962 to 1970, the SRC has "conducted foundation-funded voter registration programs in the South which placed an estimated 1.5 million blacks on registration rolls in 11 southern states."

The pace of furious activity left Twomey little time for leisure, and he had little inclination to enjoy the festive frivolities of Mardi Gras. A letter to an old friend, dean of the Law School of the University of San Francisco mentions that "Mardi Gras as usual passed without my being in the least concerned about it. As a matter of fact, I did not leave the campus during the festivities."

Though he was not a political man, Lou consistently voted for the Democratic candidate for president and shared with Adlai Stevenson the sense of pride that even lost elections could not deny. After the presidential election of 1952 he wrote Stevenson a note of condolence: "In you America has seen a vision of true greatness seldom granted to any nation." He added that "American citizens are privileged indeed to have one of your commanding spiritual and moral stature numbered among them." Quoting words of the losing candidate, Twomey commented: "I am as you 'too old to cry and too much hurt to laugh.'"

Despite the reserve Twomey manifested in public politicking, his stress on the problems of the poor brought bitter reactions from many sides. That was especially the case when he helped unorganized workers, the most deprived among whom were agricultural laborers. Specifically, the anguish of the sugar cane workers of Louisiana enlisted

Twomey's sympathy, and his endorsement of their 1953 strike lost him wide backing.

Following World War II, the head of Catholic Rural Life movement, Msgr. Luigi Ligutti, had encouraged several thousand Polish refugees to take up farming in the cane and strawberry fields of southern Louisiana. Soon, however, the refugees fled the grim conditions imposed on them. Most of the workers were black, with a yearly income between $700 and $1,000 in 1953, to support a family. At the time, the Bureau of National Affairs judged a minimum income of $3,871 for such a family.

Thanks to the leadership of Rev. Vincent O'Connell, S. M., a small Agricultural Workers Union was established, representing some 2,000 field workers. O'Connell brought in field organizers, especially Hank Hasiwar, to teach the workers collective bargaining — the first such unionization among farmers. Notice was sent the large cane growers that the workers intended to strike unless certain minimum demands were met by the employers. The main issue was, in fact, that of the right to collective bargaining.

The Agricultural Workers Union became affiliated with the AFL and began to realize strong moral support to small farmers and workers. Lou was involved with them and wrote the director of the Southern Conference of Teamsters: "There are thousands of workers on the plantations who live in a state of almost semi-feudalism. Like all other human beings they have an instinctive desire for freedom and for decent working conditions. But for generations an almost impenetrable wall of paternalism has severely limited their possibility of enjoying this freedom and decency. Of themselves they are powerless to make any effective efforts to right their pitiable condition. Strong union organization is really their only hope."

On October 12, 1953, the union struck the corporation-owned plantations which hired the majority of cane field workers. Since the land owners or, in some cases, the growers who leased the land for cane, owned nearly all the dwellings of the strikers, both the termination of lights and water use and eviction from the premises of the plantations followed quickly. The plantation operators had a powerful organization, the American Sugar Cane League, enabling them to coordinate their own response to the strike strategy. They got injunctions in the local courts to compel the strikers to desist from all strike and union activity and got Hank Hasiwar arrested more than once. Since neither the Wagner Act nor the subsequent labor legislation provided the right of the farm workers to form unions, the courts coerced the strikers to abandon their strategy. The NAWU had only scant financial resources to provide for the helpless workers and secure legal assistance. Moreover, once the injunctions became effective, the strike had no chance of succeeding that year because of the short duration of the cane harvest season. Union officials directed their members to return to work 28 days after the strike began.

Before the strike Twomey had begged funds from the Teamsters' Union for the National Agricultural Workers Union. During the strike he stayed in close contact with H. L. Mitchell, president of the union, and consulted with Rowland Watts of the Workers Defense League at Mitchell's request. After the utilities had been turned off and many families were ordered to leave their quarters, Twomey, working with Stephen and Patty Ryan, Phil and Maria Hornung and other members of the Commission on Human Rights, organized caravans of relief with clothing and food for the strikers, and considerable cash funds from Archbishop Rummel.

Time magazine reported on the strike, stating that the union workers had a "powerful ally in the Roman Catholic Church which is strong in Louisiana." The article quoted Twomey as saying: "The workers are apparently willing to take whatever risks are involved to free, if not themselves, at least their children, from this environment." Though the evidence showed that the strikers suffered rather than inflicted violence and the "risks" Twomey mentioned referred to their own security, he evoked the ire of the plantation owners.

A special file in the Twomey collection, whimsically designated "fan-pan mail," which contained four bulging folders by the end of Lou's life, became the reservoir for hostile reactions sent him or about him to others. Among the items kept were from two cane growers. S. J. Gianelloni wrote Twomey that he had on several occasions read "excerpts from speeches and various statements you have made relative to labor and social problems in Louisiana." He then charged that "most of them are creeping with loaded and slanted words and that few, if any, reflect the clear, objective and logical understanding, the patience and humility, that should come from one who is supposed to be a bearer of Christ's Word." He went on to instruct the priest-reformer: "Read the parable of Christ about the workers in the vineyard; preach the Gospel as Christ gave it to us—a Gospel of love, not of hate and violence." Written on "Longwood Plantation" stationery, the letter notified Twomey that carbon copies had been sent to the president of Loyola University and to the superior of Southern Jesuits.

Another piece of "pan" mail retained in the file came from C. A. Duplantis, Jr., via Henry Luce, editor of *Time*. The last sentence warned Twomey indirectly that: "The misled Jesuit Fathers and

Yankee carpet-baggers who could be clearing their cities of filth and vermin and rackets and narcotics instead of stirring racial hatred will have to take the responsibility for whatever happens." Since this letter was addressed to Luce, it did not call for a reply from Twomey; the first, however, elicited a typical response: "I always welcome informed, constructive criticism. Your letter is hardly based on such criticism." He then explained the circumstances of his interview with the *Time* correspondent and invited Gianelloni to a further exchange of views. The reply came with more advice for the reformer: "I have seen a great deal of what might be called poverty and ignorance about the world, but when I put myself in the mood of the country or area, I find that it is a somewhat relative thing, that these people are very poor or not very poor or very ignorant; instead they are rich in their way of life and wise in the knowledge that makes it possible for them to carry on." He insisted that "change for them must come slowly and should never be forced upon them."

For the cane workers the strike provided only a dramatic episode in an ongoing nightmare. Today they still endure the same dreary life which impelled them to attempt organized opposition in the fifties. A series of 15 articles in 1974 entitled "Behind the Cane Curtain" in the New Orleans *States-Item* further documented the bitter living conditions of the workers; so did a nationally televised documentary. Once again Father O'Connell was behind this.

Twomey never forgot the cane workers, and the long history of his involvement with them and their needs led to an invitation in 1962 from Frank Graham, former senator from North Carolina and then chairman of the National Sharecropper Fund. Graham invited Twomey to meet for a conference "to discuss how economic and social progress may be more fully shared in the rural South." Lou began to carry his message beyond Louisiana to national forums, since the NSF embraced the entire country. Despite the local failure of the cause, Twomey gained a more commanding voice as spokesman for labor and justice.

The year after the cane workers' strike failure, Lou's voice rang out in the halls of the state Legislature. During the summer of 1954 he spoke in both houses in favor of workers. At that time the issue of "right-to-work" laws dominated the attention of pro-union spokesmen. In 1935 the Wagner Act had allowed unions the right of collective bargaining. However, after numerous strikes especially in coal, railroad and steel industries during the forties, the public attitude toward unions changed. Widespread anger at the unions encouraged the passage of the Taft-Hartley Act in 1947, restricting the prerogatives of unions in negotiations with management. Further, the new national legislation made it possible for individual states to pass laws against the principle of unionism. The laws, later called "right-to-work" laws, if passed within a given state, permitted nonunion workers to remain out of unions even when the union representatives negotiated for their benefits. Seventeen states, mostly Southern, passed such laws. Louisiana was about to vote on the subject.

Archbishop Rummel of New Orleans denounced the legislation in strong terms and telegraphed the elected representatives considering the bill that during the public hearings "Rev. Louis J. Twomey of Loyola University will represent me."

Lou's close ties with such powerful spokesmen in the labor camp yielded some financial support from the unions to the Institute. Charles Winters, Teamster in Louisiana, and James O'Brien as a national representative of the United Steelworkers both directed contributions—$1,500 and $5,000 respectively. As always, however, gifts were barely sufficient to keep the Institute from financial collapse, until the Johnson administration gave some financial grants in the late sixties, shortly before Lou's death. While he was in the hospital, his secretary Lucie St. Pee wrote letters of thanks in his name. (Another dedicated secretary, Marie Bergeron, was in Fichter's words "best and most steadfast and worked for a mere pittance until her death.")

Father Twomey

Chapter 4
COMMUNISM

The years of Lou Twomey's life viewed in this chapter coincide approximately with those of the previous one. Their context, however, is different enough, we believe, to warrant distinct treatment. That context is inevitably that of the Cold War. If some of his preoccupations, and much of rhetoric, now seem dated, this should not be surprising. For though ahead of his time in his impatience to get things done, Lou was a prophet only in the sense of one who preached vigorously and unequivocally, hearlding the kingdom, summoning to repentance and change. He was, I believe, not so much a foreseer as a seer, often of now obvious but then neglected realities.

During the 1950's the most burning issue in the national mood was that of communism. Following the World War II cooperation between the United States and the Soviet Union came the McCarthy era. Gone was the euphoria of common victory. Fear of the Soviet Union and of the Communist party and ideology became simplistic, if not obsessive. Obviously, it was difficult for people working in the area of social reform to walk a tightrope between accepting the Communist position and becoming merely anti-Communist. Lou Twomey's task was, at that time, that of helping the labor movement free itself from Communist infiltration, while positively working to remove the very social ills against which communism and many leftist idealists built a persuasive case.

As a devout, orthodox Christian, Lou felt deeply the atheistic dimension of Marxism as it had been concretely applied in Soviet and other persecution of religion. Pope Pius XII, who was very much concerned about social justice, had been altogether uncompromising in his disapproval of communism and any attitude of cooperation with the movement. The Italian election of 1948, during which the Church had worked openly with other non-Communist elements to secure the defeat of the Party at the polls, showed the typical Catholic mood of the late forties and fifties. I was personally in Italy at the time and recall vividly the violence of attack and counter-attack from both sides.

Pope John had not yet appeared on the scene, nor had the Christian dialogue with Marxists been entered into, nor even seemed conceivable. Vatican Council II was far in the future, and quite unforeseeable. It would be some years before, say, Roger Garaudy's *From Anathema to Dialogue* would appear. (On the occasion of its appearance, the publishers in New York asked me to do a simultaneous translation of Garaudy's press conference; our mutual trust was even then a novel, almost thrilling experience. Some time later, to be sure, Mr. Garaudy was ousted from the party in France, ostensibly because he seemed all too willing to engage in dialogue.)

In 1957 a respected psychiatrist, Dr. William Sorum, sat before a sub-group of the House of Un-American Activities Committee in New Orleans to testify about his past membership in the Communist party. Sorum told the committee members that most of the Communist party members he had known did not consider themselves to be traitors but supporters of "a better way of life." While Sorum recommended publicly that other people who had been members of the Communist party "admit their membership and get it off their chest," he also told the committee that the hearing left him little satisfaction. His testimony made front-page news.

Lou Twomey was very much involved as a counselor to Dr. Sorum, though this did not appear in the public press. Sorum was trying not to damage the reputations of respected citizens who had abandoned the Communist ideology as a vehicle for legitimate reform. Both priest and psychiatrist knew that decent reform-minded people had joined the party in an honest endeavor to improve society. Both granted that communism had a tantalizing appeal for anyone concerned with social problems. Twomey, however, had consistently denounced the appeal as a "siren snare" of a doctrine inherently opposed to God's glory and mankind's true dignity. Both Dr. Sorum and Lou defended the integrity of loyal Americans who had been lured into Communist identification in pursuit of justice.

The opposing ideas of communism and religion, the problem of a common endeavor of reform in the social order, and the strong public debate over Communist subversion at mid-century, put Twomey on a collision course with exponents of the Marxist ideology. He understood the clash was inevitable and quickly took his stand as a reformer implacably opposed to the Communist movement. His stance demanded a delicate sense of balance, since he sympathized with the reform impetus, while repudiating the doctrine and methodology of the Communists themselves. Both doctrinaire leftists and intransigent conservatives often tried to topple the equilibrium Twomey maintained in his confrontation.

In a course on communism which he taught Lou examined the Marxist underpinning of communism and demonstrated its incompatibility with orthodox Christianity. According to Marxist theory, matter alone is real. Hegelians had conceived of nature as "merely the 'alienation of the absolute idea', so to say, a degradation of the idea." Feuerbach reversed the relation of cause and effect, contending that matter effected ideas. He taught that material nature, existing uncaused and eternally produced through its inherent attribute, motion, any form of life or consequent human activity. Therefore, philosophy and "higher beings which our religious fantasies have created are only the fantastic reflection of our own essence," as Lou interpreted Feuerbach's system. Marxism denied the need for any causality outside of the material universe. Moral choice, as founded on a conviction about man as immortal, was meaningless.

Dialectical materialism, as Twomey understood it, denied that man could claim any more dignity as a being than that of having arrived at the highest state in an ongoing process of developing history. The only absolute truth was that the process inevitably moved man forward. Despite the advance man had made in this deterministic process, Marxists argued that no "completely human society has ever yet existed." An essential step in the march of history toward the ideal society required the abolition of private ownership of property. Marxism thus militated against Lou's convictions about the dignity of man: free will meant nothing, tradition had no importance, and non-Hegelian metaphysics was an illusion.

All exponents of the Communist doctrine did more than simply deny the possibility of transcendence; they explicitly rejected religion and the deity worshiped in the Judaeo-Christian heritage. Further, they manifested their rejection in action. Twomey often quoted Lenin's assertion that "all religious ideas, all ideas about any little god, even of flirting with a little god, are an unspeakable abomination." He cited Marx, too, as declaring: "I hate the gods." Obviously, such militant atheism could not possibly offer a viable premise for man seeking to solve social problems. (I recall my surprise when Roger Garaudy told me that "after Pope John and Vatican Council II, Marx would not have smelt opium so much in Christianity.")

In addition to the materialism and determinism of communism, Lou found hubris as well, since it taught that man needed no assistance outside himself, hence no need for grace. Further, the ethics of communism allowed men the use of aggressive violence to foster movement in the historical process. Such activity was moral, the Communist argued, since it brought the necessary alteration in the control of power.

Twomey's analysis, while hardly satisfying professional philosophers, was by no means based on casual knowledge. I have examined his library, still left intact, and found three large shelves of books about communism, not all mere popularizations. Dr. Sorum, who had taught in official party schools, judges that Lou possessed a "sophisticated grasp of Communist teaching."

The first public attacks Twomey made on communism in 1946 were reported in the St. Louis *Globe Democrat* (January 24 and February 15). Using a belligerent diction which he would later abandon, he charged that "communism strives to cloak its sinister purposes with the outer trappings of respectability by a hypocritical use of democratic phraseology." He went on to label the movement as "a godless, ruthless, anti-democratic and essentially inhuman totalitarianism." He told the Kiwanis Club that "communism was even more despicable than was the horrid aberration of Nazism." To the Co-operative Club in St. Louis he asserted that "Russia is consolidating her position by the identical methods used by Hitler." The blame for our failure to prevent such developments, he stated, could be found in the "State Department with its weasel words of diplomatic camouflage." This was not all: "Instead of statesmanship, we get filibusters engineered by small-minded politicians, national scandals precipitated by party politics, near chaos erupting in industrial disputes, special interests taking priority over the common welfare. We plead for and we desperately need enlightened leadership and we get a sickening combination of self-seeking and gross incompetency." The acerbic tone in these early days seems more reminiscent of Father Coughlin than of the later Lou Twomey.

When Lou founded the Institute at Loyola in 1947 he remained staunchly opposed to communism, while rarely using the strong language that marked his early attacks. At Loyola the college paper spoke of him as an "anti-communist," and Lou invited a crusading former F.B.I. agent to speak to the students on the evils of communism. But he tended to concentrate more and more on the failure of Christians and capitalists to offer attractive reform for the oppressed and exploited, who easily turned to the Communists as liberators, only to suffer new disillusionment.

During the Alger Hiss case Lou had to take a stand. He had attended Georgetown University with Thomas Murphy, who successfully prosecuted Hiss in 1950 for perjury in denying that he served as a Communist agent while employed by the State Department. Twomey wrote

Murphy and assured him that "though you will receive hundreds, not to say thousands, of richly-merited congratulatory messages on the magnificent job, yet I think that none will be more sincere than my own." At the same time, Lou felt that McCarthy was a dangerous fanatic.

With his interest in unions, Lou was particularly concerned about Communist influence in them. While studying in St. Louis he met Angelo Verdu, then an official of the International Union of Mine-Mill and Smelter Workers. This was an affiliate of the Congress of Industrial Organizations. Verdu corresponded with Twomey after their meeting and gave him information about Communist associations within the union. Verdu later left that union to join one associated with the CIO and kept Lou posted on the major anti-Communist activities of the CIO. He described in detail the CIO reception of George Marshall, Philip Murray's attacks on the Communists, and the rise of the anti-Communist Walter Reuther. This was at the very time that his future friend and associate, William Sorum, was working to organize for the Communist party within the ranks of CIO members.

At the same time, anti-Communists of the extreme right took little comfort in Lou's frequent criticism of the injustice in American society and other nations that claimed the Judaeo-Christian heritage. While attacking communism, he delivered many a critique of the failures of capitalism. He enjoyed quoting Maurice J. Tobin, Secretary of Labor, who had told a group of fellow Catholics: "I can assure you that Communists are not slow to point out to the poor fish who nibble at their line the difference between moral teachings outlined in the papal encyclicals and Christian conduct."

In 1949 Lou received considerable support from a letter written to all Jesuits by their superior general in Rome, John Baptist Janssens, S.J. The letter was titled "De Apostolatu Sociali" ("On the Social Apostolate"), and Lou used it as a mandate exhorting his brother Jesuits to struggle boldly in the effort to transform society. He agreed with Father Janssens that the only effective alternative to a tyranny of the human spirit by communism was a society which acknowledged, protected and respected the dignity of the person in a just and humane environment.

As a person scrupulously observant of the directives of his religious superiors, Lou found this letter a great boost to his morale. He eagerly quoted the letter in the *Blueprint,* especially the passage that follows: "As long as Christ, in our least brethren, suffers injustice, is treated harshly; as long as hatred prevails among men and classes of men, it is not lawful for any priest or religious, nay even for any Christian, to rest from his labors. Even if Communism or any other form of materialism did not threaten and persecute the Church, it would be incumbent upon us to come to the aid of our brothers in Christ by struggling for a more equitable distribution of goods both material and spiritual." The letter went on to urge Jesuits to study the papal social encyclicals and strive to effect their implementation. Lou wrote more than 30 essays urging the use of Jesuit manpower at all levels in the work of the social apostolate. A younger Jesuit recalls that after one of Lou's talks in the seminary, his classmates were so impressed that many wanted to change their academic specialties and become sociologists or social workers.

Another person strongly influenced Lou's approach to communism, Dr. Charles Malik, representative of Lebanon to the United Nations. His 1949 address to the United Nations, "War and Peace," became a favorite source of materials for the *Blueprint*. After trenchant criticisms of communism, Dr. Malik insisted that "war and peace are not only a function of communism; they depend also on the state of health and illness in Western culture." He enumerated "phases of Western life which are repulsively materialistic," adding that "the spirit of business and gain, the maddening variety of things exciting your concupiscence, the utter selfishness of uncoordinated activity does not attract and inspire." For people trying to choose between "the soulless materialism of the West and the militant materialism of the East, it was possible that the love and truth are still at the heart of the West" will easily be obscured. The critique submitted by Malik, a professed Christian and pro-Western, left anti-Communist listeners little comfort and no sense of triumph.

Twomey agreed that Malik's reasons for the inability of the West to appeal to the uncommitted nations explained the success of the Communist movement. Malik denied that the ideas of communism were true and he thought communists' commitment "misguided," but he found no "comparable ideological passion in the West."

Another thinker who impressed Lou was Douglas Hyde, a former dedicated communist and editor of the London *Daily Worker*. His volume, *I Believed,* published in 1950, became a kind of secular bible for Twomey when he advocated reform instead of virulent negativism. Hyde had stressed that often the people who joined the Communist movement were the most idealistic and not malicious. He argued, too, that communism "had its origins in precisely that spiritual vacuum which exists all over what was once Christendom. Both Twomey and Hyde were enthusiastic when Pope John published his encyclical *Mater et Magistra* in 1961.

This remarkable encyclical departed little from earlier papal documents. But it did make them more explicit and more adapted to the present. It stressed the right of every person, whether employer or employee, to representation at all levels of economic life. It also stressed the responsibilities of nations to act in concert for the welfare of all humanity. What struck Lou immediately was that though the encyclical was "the longest in the history of the Church, in the entire document the Pope mentions communism only once—and that in passing." This he interpreted to mean that "John XXIII is telling us to quit pushing the panic button and to be quick about the removal of social evils in which communism got started."

In 1961 Lou collaborated with a Jesuit writer, William B. Faherty, in a pamphlet on the topic of communism: *Questions and Answers on Communism*. Within two years 45,051 copies were sold. Here, as in copies of the *Blueprint* the stress was on the positive need of reform rather than on a negative crusade.

In advocating reform Twomey spared no one, least of all his fellow Catholics. He pointed out that communism had made its strongest appeal in the free world in countries at least nominally Catholic. He sympathized with the destitute of those countries and indicted complacent Catholics, especially the clergy: "As long as poverty and illiteracy scourge the overwhelming percentage of the masses in these countries; as long as the very few at the top can enjoy material comfort at the expense of the very many at the bottom; as long as this vast discrepancy is not only tolerated but abetted by churchmen, just so long will 'the humble people' swell the burgeoning ranks of the ill-fed, the ill-clothed, the ill-housed who seek hope in communism because they have been too blinded by the injustice and uncharity of their Christian overlords to see any Christianity."

He had equally trenchant criticism for his fellow Americans who ignored the plight of the poor. "We have become complacent in our own physical well-being," he wrote a friend, "and even callow toward the suffering of those less fortunate than we." Nevertheless, he remained confident that a fundamental decency still characterized Americans generally. "Beneath the wounds inflicted on the West and on America by rank materialism, which sacrifices the higher values of the intellect to the groveling demands of the senses," he added, "there still lie a sound body and a noble soul."

It goes without saying that Lou made enemies, very often among staunch anti-Communists. His evident sincerity and constructive proposals had convinced William Sorum and others that at least some non-Communists energetically pursued reform. To them, the programs advocated by Twomey provided a concrete alternative to the Communist transformation of society. But among ardent patriots who found any criticism of the status quo tantamount to treason, he was *persona non grata*.

William Buckley, editor of *National Review* and a well known Catholic, dismissed Pope John's encyclical *Mater et Magistra* with the quip "Mater, si; Magistra no." He denied that the Pope had the right to give Catholics the advice contained in the encyclical and that the advice itself offered a wise course for anyone or any nation. This naturally offended such a loyal Catholic as Lou Twomey. The "flippancy" of Buckley's boutade, he felt, was "unworthy of high quality journalism." When Buckley dubbed the encyclical "a venture in triviality," Twomey wrote in the *Blueprint* that he found the remark "incredible and peevish."

Buckley, in turn, wrote an article in a popular Catholic magazine, *Ave Maria*, in 1962, in which he pointedly criticized Twomey and his policy of responding to the success of communism. He debated the argument Twomey presented to an audience at Notre Dame University. He argued that Twomey's claim that Communists had advanced "because of our supreme unconcern with gross violations of justice and charity here and abroad" was "nonsensical." He did not deny that secular society should promote justice; rather, he argued that "the temptation of the liberal is to secularize a uniquely religious relationship." While admitting that "every act of justice causes the heavenly chorus to rejoice," Buckley argued that "a correlation has never been established between the extent of injustice and the appeal of communism." He further contested the relevance of Twomey's recommended strategy that the best defense against communism was an offensive campaign for justice.

Twomey quoted John Foster Dulles to the effect that "our greatest national scandal and our most dangerous international hazard" was racial discrimination. Buckley rejected the argument that segregationists indirectly supported those who opposed America and replied that "the single greatest encouragement to international communism is the existence of a class of people who can make that kind of statement." Further he maintained that "the so-called social reforms which Father Twomey has so much desired" did nothing at all to limit the growth of communism.

Donald Thorman, then the editor of *Ave Maria*, invited Twomey to reply. Though Thorman and Twomey had been friends for years, Twomey wrote that he saw little value in engaging in public debate with Buckley and felt that it "would lead to an unending series of articles and counter-articles." I, for one, would have enjoyed such a series between debaters of such stature.

Of all the charges made against people reputedly pro-Communist, none seems more strange than the allegation that Twomey himself was a Communist agitator. Yet it was not primarily in self-defense that Lou often wrote against those who made unsubstantiated assaults on those who may not have appeared sufficiently anti-Communist: "The reckless practice of throwing around unsubstantiated charges of treason against outstanding personalities in political and civic life is a serious violation (objectively at least) of the 8th Commandment." He quoted the editor of *The Sign* magazine that "those Catholics who follow the line set by *The National Review*, Father Ginder (then editor of the Catholic weekly, *The Sunday Visitor*), Barry Goldwater, the John Birch Society" might be shocked "to find that the Pope teaches what they have been accustomed to condemn as 'liberal'."

He felt that it was important for the Catholic Church to renounce identification with the negative "anti-Communists." For this reason he collaborated with Louis Gales and Fred Barnes of the *Catholic Digest* Corporation to analyze a popular anti-Communist film, "Operation Abolition." Lou narrated another film entitled "Autopsy On Operation Abolition," dispassionately examining the ground for many of the alarmist statements made in the other film. Russel W. Gibbons, secretary of the Catholic Council on Civil Liberties, judged that Twomey had demonstrated the complexity of the situations portrayed and confounded any simplistic interpretations.

At the same time, Lou never once suggested that one could trust the Communist party leadership. He defended the need of a strong military system in the free world and considered naive those who accepted the call for peaceful coexistence as justifying unilateral disarmament. He wrote specifically of the danger of "the possibility of letting down both our ideological and military guard."

In his struggle to effect social reform, Twomey often stated that communism—as "an effect rather than a cause"—was "rushing in to fill the voids created in men's souls as well as their stomachs by the failure of the West." Lou was profoundly concerned about both voids.

Father Twomey and staff, Bernard J. Offerman and B. Raynal Ariatti

Chapter 5
RACE

When Lou Twomey came to New Orleans to work at Loyola University in 1947, the city, for all its elegance, was still very much a white person's enclave. While blacks could ride the St. Charles Avenue trolley and other public conveyances, they were rigorously segregated into the back seats. Even Audubon Park was for whites only, and when integration orders were imposed, the city closed the Audubon swimming pool for some years rather than allow blacks and whites to swim together. I vividly recall visiting New Orleans at that time and meeting a black priest friend at the railway station; there was literally no public place where we could legally sit together in the entire city. When I tell this to college-age blacks today, or whites for that matter, they find it hard to believe.

The United States Department of Labor and the National Catholic Welfare Conference often arranged for Lou Twomey to host their guests. Particularly when either agency entertained black guests in New Orleans they relied on him to provide hospitality that would embarrass no one. This required tact and discretion to protect the dignity of those being welcomed. For this, Twomey depended on loyal and daring friends, like lawyers John Nelson and Ivor Trapolin, Dr. William Sorum and novelist Walker Percy. Years later these friends recall the drama involved in extending simple courtesy in racially mixed social gatherings.

One such occasion came as late as 1957. Alioune Diop, distinguished author and editor of the newspaper *Présence Africaine* in Senegal, was to visit New Orleans. Vincent Allen of the State Department and Robert Murphy of NCWC asked Twomey to take care of the black visitor. Since the city's hotels were still segregated, Lou was to make housing accomodations and arrange for tours, meetings, and in this case a formal cocktail party at the Trapolin home. The Trapolins live in the fashionable "uptown" area and enjoy prestige in New Orleans society. Walker Percy describes Ivor Trapolin as, at the time, "a young, struggling lawyer with a large family who displayed enormous cour-

age by inviting a racially mixed group to his home."
Other friends, like John and Marie Nelson, did much of this entertaining at no small personal risk. So did Stephen and Patty Ryan, Professor and Mrs. Numa Rousseve, and other generous members of the faculty of Xavier University, both black and white. Neighbors of the Nelsons, in fact, quit speaking to them.

At about this time racists banded together in "White Citizens' Councils." Twomey wrote Bishop (now Cardinal) John Wright in 1956 reporting that at one of these Council meetings, "I had the honor of having my name loudly booed." He added that "after the meeting a fiery cross was burned in front of Archbishop Rummel's residence." The same twisted ceremony greeted the integration of Spring Hill College (Mobile, Alabama) at about this time, when that college was integrated by Andrew C. Smith, S.J. Indeed, his associate, Albert S. Foley, S.J., barely escaped physical violence from the Ku Klux Klan.

Twomey's long and consistent advocacy of justice for black people insured his position as a target of segregationists' ire and attacks. Dr. Daniel Thompson, a black educator at Dillard University and author of *The Negro Leadership Class*, worked closely with Lou in his efforts. "No one can appreciate Father Twomey's contributions to the blacks," he told us, "unless they understand the times in which he lived." He made a particularly significant observation after this: "One word then in defense of racial equality and desegregation was worth more than reams and volumes of statements articulated later by civil rights advocates." Dr. Thompson then added: "To put it in scriptural terms, Twomey was a voice crying in the wilderness. He was one of the greatest leaders New Orleans has ever had."

Leadership in the cause of racial justice did not come naturally to a Southern white. Lou had accepted segregation of the races as a normal pattern of interaction between black and white people. In 1963 he gave an autobiographical address over radio, recalling how his attitude had changed: "I was born and grew up in a rigidly segregated Southern community. As a boy and later as a young man I accepted segregated patterns in political, economic, education, cultural, and even religious life as I did the air I breathed." He took for granted that "Negroes should be excluded from white hotels, restaurants and theatres; that they should be off limits in parks and other public facilities, and should, in a word 'keep their place.' "

In this talk, Lou did not spare his educators. "The intellectual and moral development I acquired was certainly not accompanied by even elementary understanding of the serious wrongfulness of my ideas and practices in race relations." At some point, very likely during his years of special study (1945-1947), his thinking changed and he came to detest racial segregation: "Exactly when, I cannot say, but eventually I began to be less and less complacent with the community's and my own callous acceptance of the sufferings inflicted on the Negro through compulsory segregation." He went so far as to compare the crime of racism to murder: "I was not taught that the deliberate and willful denial of the necessities for a truly human life is also murder —in this instance, slow murder. In the context of race relations in the United States and generally throughout the Western world, this crime victimizes an entire race."

Back in 1948 he had already spoken out strongly on the subject, offering his credentials as a Southerner: "I should like to state that I am a Southerner, born and raised in the South and proud of most of our Southern traditions. Furthermore, I qualify as a Southerner on the further score that I had my great-grandfather and five great uncles killed fighting for the South during the Civil War . . . I cannot be charged with being a 'Yankee intruder.'"

This was not merely a rhetorical ploy. He showed genuine understanding and sympathy regarding the South: "The Civil War left the South politically powerless, economically improverished and socially bewildered," he wrote in 1956. He argued that the South needed "a sympathetic understanding to recover and rehabilitate itself. Instead, from 1865 to 1877 it was given mostly salt for its wounds. As a consequence of that past, attitudes such as blind loyalty to everything Southern, instinctive resistance to 'outside interference,' extreme sensitiveness to criticism, and worst of all a deep-rooted advocacy of white supremacy with a dogged defense of segregation" were accepted as properly Southern.

The cause of racial justice, like the other causes for which he labored, led Twomey to practical tactics. Fortunately, the integration of classes at the Institute of Human Relations needed no other authority than his own. While the Institute gave certificates, names did not go to the university registrar. He simply deliberated with his staff and then resolved to accept all applicants. Loyola University at the time was still all-white, as were all other white public and private accredited schools in Louisiana. New Orleans had the only black Catholic institution of higher education in the United States, Xavier University, and Lou helped Xavier graduates enter law schools, first at Georgetown University, then at Loyola.

A 1949 Xavier graduate, Harry Alexander, who had been the first president of the interracial intercollegiate group, impressed Lou very favorably. In a letter of recommendation to the Georgetown law school, Lou explained that Alexander had applied first to Loyola. "He had given arguments for his admission which we simply could not answer, and yet we are in the position of having to refuse Negro applicants." Francis Lucey, S.J., Regent of the Law School at Georgetown, wrote Lou that Harry Alexander was accepted and that "your interest in the young man had much weight in the decision." After receiving his law degree, Alexander was appointed a federal judge for Washington, D.C.

Another Xavier graduate whom Lou helped to enter the Georgetown law school was Richard Gumble. At Lou's advice, Gumble had applied to Loyola and might well have been accepted. A student gathering, however, was strong in protest and the administration yielded. Numa Rousseve (professor at Xavier University and long associated with Lou in the movement for racial justice) recalls the episode clearly: "The students used as a pretext the danger of Loyola's small law school going under, with the behemoth—Tulane—next door. But the real reason—the real reason, as I know from some of the students—was that they were afraid Gumble's admission would raise the academic curve and make it hard for some of them to pass. So, despite Father Twomey, the administration yielded to student pressure."

By 1952, however, when the Loyola Law School had become desegregated, Gumble had already started at Georgetown. Lou asked him to transfer back to New Orleans. Gumble thanked Lou, asserting that "you were one of the few I knew who were sincere, and I would be extremely hurt if you felt all your efforts have been in vain. Please believe me when I say that deep down in my heart I wish that I were at home, but when I think of all I have stated, I cannot follow my heart—I must follow my head." Gumble graduated from Georgetown and went to to become a distinguished federal judge.

Two young black men encouraged by Twomey did break the race barrier by attending Law School at Loyola and then going on to gain respected positions in the academic and business worlds of New Orleans. As mentioned earlier, these were Norman Francis and Benjamin Johnson. Lou, as Regent of the Law School, pleaded their case to W. Patrick Donnelly, S.J., then president of Loyola, who gave the needed permission. It was several years before the undergraduate program at Loyola was open to blacks. (In 1958, when I was appointed dean of the Loyola College of Music, I followed Lou's example and admitted the first black. This demanded no special courage, since the faculty had no opposition, and when I checked with the student president I was assured that "musicians haven't any problems; we're used to playing together.")

Meantime, of course, Lou preached publicly on race, wrote letters of recommendation for black students, and castigated racist literature. His personal friendship with blacks deepened his sensitivity in their regard. He was very critical of black-faced minstrel shows as offensive to blacks. (I recall that his friend, Albert S. Foley, S.J., had done as much in Kansas back in the early 1940's and was harshly judged at the time.) Dr. Daniel Thompson recalls that no one ever used derogatory terms like "Spic" or "Nigger" or "Kike" in Lou's presence; "his very presence made that impossible."

Of all issues involving race, none evoked a stronger emotional reaction than that of interracial marriage. "Sooner or later in any discussion of race relations," Lou wrote, "someone almost invariably will come up with the perennial 'Would you want your sister to marry a Negro?'" He explained that neither faith nor philosophy had any problem about interracial marriage, but with a strong realization of practical matters he explained that present circumstances in America put serious obstacles in the way of success and warned of hardships which inevitably accompany the partners. "The social censure in modern American society (1951) visited upon the parties and their children is so severe that relatively few racially mixed couples maintain happiness." Nevertheless, he defended the right of couples to enter into mixed interracial marriages, "having reviewed and understood the hardships involved."

Explosive reactions came from both sides. A nun commented that Lou's caution vitiated the whole argument made for racial justice. Patiently Lou replied, repeating his argument in slightly different terms. On the other hand, a mother of two missionary priests wrote in indignation that intermarriage will bring about a state where "the white race will be no more."

Once again Lou's eloquence proved a powerful asset, as he spoke in churches, schools and the halls of labor unions. He joined ranks with other citizens in organizations such as the Urban League and the National Association for the Advancement of Colored People. Some of his most significant work on race was done with the labor unions.

Lou gave the keynote address at the 1953 meeting of the Southern Conference of the Teamsters' Union in Biloxi, Mississippi. He reviewed the history of the hard struggle of the men who organized the labor movement. He showed the justice of their cause. Having made them benevolent, he addressed the union men on the need of supporting the cane workers of Louisiana (as seen in a previous chapter) and challenged them to face the problem of racial discrimination.

As usual, Twomey appealed both to Christian morality and to enlightened self-interest, condemning segregation on both grounds. He quoted a remark of Adlai Stevenson made in a speech in New Orleans in 1952: "all of us most certainly regret the tragedy of even having to talk about human rights after 2,000 years of Christianity." He developed the theme in a characteristic way: "My principal interest in the labor movement is my interest in human beings. I believe that all inspiration in the labor movement should find its source in concern for the dignity of man." That dignity entitled every human person to rights which were "God-given," and which should "enable him to command all those means, material and spiritual, which are necessary for him to live in accordance with his human dignity." The very claims that protected the cause of unions obtained equally for agricultural workers and victims of racial discrimination.

Lou kept in close touch with the Southern Conference of Teamsters for the rest of his life, and it is somehow appropriate that his very last public address, delivered shortly before he died in 1969, was to that group. Again he appealed for dedication to eliminating racial discrimination. This time he spoke also of Cesar Chavez and told the Teamsters that "there was something wrong" in the failure of industrial unions to give aid to the farm workers.

Another speech to union people in Baton Rouge, November 21, 1955, gained international press coverage, bringing praise and blame and requests for reprints from Canada and Hong Kong.

Two confidential reports available to Twomey in 1956 and 1957 proved rather discouraging. One came from the Southern Regional Council dealing with anti-union people in White Citizens' Councils in several states. The other, prepared for the executive board of the Jewish Labor Committee National Trade Union Council showed that most union members in the South were against school integration. This stressed racial tensions within the labor movement. Further, in almost half of fifty locals with racial strife, there were union members who also belonged to White Citizens' Councils. One of the most disquieting developments in the South since the Supreme Court decision outlawing segregated public schools is the reaction among union men, Twomey wrote. Most distressing to him was the fact that "a seeming majority of the rank and file place higher priority on their 'loyalty' to the White Citizens' Councils than on their loyalty to their unions."

Lou's struggle to bring the Catholic Church in New Orleans into the battle for racial equality gained official Jesuit sanction in 1954. A. William Crandell, S.J., then superior of the Southern Jesuits, issued a letter giving norms for integrating all Jesuit schools, parishes and retreat houses. While Crandell credited Twomey for much of the work leading to this decision, the timing of the letter, coming as it did after the Supreme Court ruling, was awkward. However, the letter concluded unambiguously as to the evil of segregation: "We must say that race segregation, based solely on race, is seriously immoral and, therefore, may not be approved by a Catholic."

Crandell was a cautious man and acknowledged that "I am under no delusions that everything I have said will meet with your unqualified and enthusiastic assent; however, I do expect, as a result of careful adherence to the principles, policy and program outlined in this letter a marked improvement in uniformity of doctrine, in the avoidance of extreme statements on one side or the other." Twomey made the letter available to all readers of the *Blueprint*, stipulating that it was meant exclusively for Jesuit readers. Actual implementation of the directives would, of course, require some years because of personal and institutional bias.

Additional support came from Archbishop Rummel in an official letter to "All Catholics of the Archdiocese of New Orleans" on March 15, 1953. Three years later came a bold and direct excoriation of racial segregation from the 79-year-old churchman. "This is an age when most people sit around in their felt slippers and take things easy," Twomey wrote Father John Cronin of the National Catholic Welfare Conference. Alistaire Cooke, British correspondent for the (Manchester) *Guardian* wrote an article for the Chicago *Sun-Times* praising Archbishop Rummel's stand and citing the exceptionally humane guidance given the Catholic community by the Catholic Committee of the South and the Jesuits, who "have long been active in promoting interracial councils and getting race relations discussed in parents' clubs, parish meetings, and societies pledged to certain devotions."

Opposition to the Archbishop was both covert and sometimes violent. This is hardly the place to repeat what Father Fichter has treated authoritatively in his *One-Man Research*. In the New York *Times* for July 8, 1959, John Wicklein wrote a full page report titled "Catholic Archbishop Backs New Orleans Integration." In it we read: "The Rev. Joseph Fichter, a Jesuit priest, has written books and worked actively against segregation. The Rev. Louis J. Twomey, also on the Loyola staff, is a widely known labor priest who has helped to desegregate unions in the area."

Back in 1947 the Board of Directors of Loyola University—all of them at the time Jesuits—expressed anxiety about Fichter's activity: "The thought of the Board was that while we want to avoid any prejudice against the Negro race, we feel that Father Fichter is moving entirely too fast in view of conditions here in the city." Several months later another entry in the minutes of the Board again reported: "The Board felt that Father Fichter had pushed the matter of racial relations too far and without getting necessary authorization from the president and dean." The specific issues involved racial mixing in intercollegiate student associations and the use of black speakers on the university campus. The legend of Jesuit monolithic thinking and acting was violently exploded over the race issue, and it was only eight years after the official mandate of 1954 that Loyola University integrated all classes.

One of the main roles of the Institute of Human Relations in the service of Jesuits and other Catholic educators was that of constantly circulating relevant literature. Somehow, despite set-backs and apathy on the part of those from whom he expected more, Lou Twomey remained publicly optimistic. In 1956 in an article published in *Commonweal*, "Challenge to America," he asked: "What is the basis for this optimism?" He submitted two reasons: "most Southerners have for generations taken for granted the political, economic, and social patterns which assigned the Negro a second-class status." Yet now, he stated, "the Southern conscience, despite all appearances, is profoundly disturbed." Secondly, in consequence of the upheaval in race relations, "an intensive educational process" was taking place. He maintained that this process was "taking place around crackerbarrels in country stores, in the setting of professional organizations and fashionable social clubs, on street corners, at the family dinner table." But most important for Twomey that educational process came "in formal lectures, from the pulpit and in the classroom."

He meant to complement that developing understanding through literature made available through the offices of the Institute. Each month, in the column of the *Blueprint* labeled "For the Asking," he offered four or five timely articles or reprints. Among these pamphlets were *The Teacher Approach to Social Formation* and *Social Formation Through the Regular Curriculum* (by Emmett M. Bienvenu, S.J., but as the author assures me, considerably rewritten by Lou to add rhetorical force); *The Church and Integration*, (by Harold Cooper, S.J.); two pamphlets of mine published by the American Press, *Let's Talk Sense About the Negro* and *What Do They Want Now?; An Interview with John LaFarge* (by James O'Gard); *Racism: A God-damned Thing* (by William J. Kenealy, S.J.). When the American bishops made a joint declaration condemning racial segregation entitled "Discrimination and the Christian Conscience," Lou happily wrote that "via the *Blueprint* we have distributed over 50,000 copies of the Bishops' great document." (At the same time, he often complained to me that people were happy to receive material but seldom "fed the kitty.")

The medium of radio served Twomey as an instrument especially suited to his gift of eloquence. Each Sunday for five successive weeks in June, 1958, he delivered an address over the American Broadcasting Corporation network on race, as we mentioned previously. In 1957 the national convention of the inter-faith Religious Education Association brought together leading religious thinkers from all of North America to explore "the image of man in current culture." Lou was invited to present a paper. In "To Be Treated Like a Man," he defended the thesis that man's dignity rested upon a guarantee of respect for inalienable rights inherent in the human person. Throughout the address Lou attacked racial segregation as an affront to man's dignity. His address was used as the concluding chapter of the published version of the convention's principal papers.

In the mid-fifties the school desegregation issue had become serious in New Orleans. Federal District Judge J. Skelly Wright required school boards to prepare for integration "with all deliberate speed." It was some years before the final rulings of the Supreme Court, in 1961, upheld the judgment of Judge Wright and declared all segregation laws in Louisiana unconstitutional. The fact that Wright was a Loyola graduate pleased Lou as much as the presence of Loyola graduates in the opposition distressed him. He was ashamed, too, of the footdragging of the Church schools.

In 1958 he persuaded his close friend John Nelson to run for a place on the school board then held by segregationist Emile Wagner, Jr. Lou wrote his friend Thurston Davis, S.J., editor of *America* magazine that he had "never before been so deeply committed to the backing of a candidate." Nelson described the venture as "flirtation with martyrdom" and insisted that had it not been for Twomey, whom he "regarded as a saint, making it clear that the alternative to not running for office was that of facing eternal perdition," he would have refused the quixotic adventure. (Lou could indulge in overstatement.) Both worked hard, but Nelson lost the election.

The following year, in response to an article on segregation in the South in *Jubilee* magazine, Emile Wagner had much to say about Lou Twomey, Typical was this passage: "I am always amused at the proud arrogance of so many of the zealous and rabid integrationists, you included, who consider themselves as having 'a private pipe-line to the Holy Ghost.' Such a one is Father Louis J. Twomey, S.J., whom

I know and fundamentally like, despite his emotional imbalance." (The business of the excommunication of some of Wagner's friends is complex and has been treated in Fichter's *One-Man Research*; here he states on page 107 that "Father Louis Twomey and I visited the archbishop and urged that he excommunicate the guilty persons"—not precisely Emile Wagner. Fichter adds: "The penalty of excommunication was indeed imposed, but only when it seemed too late, and for the wrong reasons." It should be recalled that Archbishop Rummel's position was particularly delicate. As a churchman he was very concerned about the possibility of causing a schism. The fact that his life was threatened some seventy times (we have this from the archdiocesan archivist) was probably of little concern to him, as he continued a policy of what some have felt to be too prudent. Historians of the entire history of church participation in the racial issues of the 1950's and 1960's have a great deal of research to do before coming to a definitive evaluation. We, of course, are only treating Lou Twomey's role.

I asked Professor Numa Rousseve, who had been intimately involved during these crucial years, whether Lou Twomey played the biggest part of all. His judicious answer merits quotation: "It's hard to say. Father Fichter was working with his sociological approach. Father Twomey was certainly one of the most important—mainly from the legal aspect. Father Vincent O'Connell did most important work in the seminary. I would be rather reluctant to assess. Each of them played a major role. But I think in the blending of the work of these three men the work got done. Father O'Connell was fiery, Father Fichter incisive, Father Twomey—well, what the Italians call dolce—but never weak, never weak."

Chapter 6
EVALUATION

Biographers always find it tempting to fit a remarkable person neatly into convenient categories, suggesting a consistency and undeviating pattern of behavior seldom if ever found in real life. Friends of Lou Twomey, at least those who lived in close quarters with him, know that he cannot be described as a supergenius who saw his mission in a flash of instant insight early in life and then carried it out sure of each step.

Even in the matter of race relations his vision was not always clear. In 1943, for example, he still wondered about the question of whether the curse of Ham might not possibly be the cause of Negroes' difficulty. This I would find quite impossible to believe except for the word of his friend Father Anthony C. O'Flynn, which I consider unimpeachable. In 1946, a year before he came to Loyola, he told students of theology at St. Marys, Kansas, that he wasn't sure whether Negroes would be admitted to the Institute of Industrial Relations. As late as 1952 he pushed for union contracts for a new building at Loyola, even though Negroes were excluded from that union.

Yet, very shortly after that, Lou changed certain priorities, confiding to a close friend that he now felt racial equality to be more important than unions. At least from the early fifties he was in the forefront of the racial battle. The particular focus of his energies did indeed change, as he saw the needs of the moment. Long before most American spokesmen he expressed concern over poverty in the world and its disastrous effects. If a single thread ran through most of his speeches and writings, it had to do with the dignity of the human person.

"Since Southerners do not respect federal authority, they must be made to fear it." This characteristic statement of Lou's appears in the lead article in *Sign* magazine for October, 1961. In "Two Southerners Speak Their Minds," Douglas J. Roche, interviewed Twomey and John Nelson. Both stressed that only the power of the federal government could really change racial matters. Nelson's statement is analogous: "The change is not going to come from within people; it will

Lindsay Williams, Vice President, Seafarers International Union and Father Twomey at banquet honoring Father Twomey

have to come from without." At the same time Lou assured Roche that he was optimistic and listed advances made toward full acceptance of blacks in American life: the work of Dr. Martin Luther King, Jr., desegregation in Southern universities; progress in voter registration; the fact that where segregation had been abolished in public affairs amicable social life had been proven possible.

As one who firmly believed in law, Lou understood the efforts of Dr. Martin Luther King, Jr., and his policy of passive resistance to gain legal rights and oppose unconstitutional bans. Consistently, however, he felt deeply frustrated by those activists who violated law to secure reform. Though he sympathized with the pain felt by people who became rioters, he could not condone their violence. In the September, 1967, *Blueprint* he wrote of the futility and evil of mob violence, the burning and looting that followed in places like Newark and Detroit. Appealing to the wisdom of Martin Luther King in his rejection of such means, Twomey quoted: "We who fought so long and so hard to achieve justice for all Americans have consistently opposed violence as a means of redress. Riots have proved ineffective, disruptive and highly damaging to the Negro population, to the civil rights cause, and to the entire nation."

It is interesting but probably idle to speculate how these two lovers of mankind might have gotten along together had they been friends. Both passionately loved justice and freedom, both had similar dreams, both were master orators endowed with a high measure of charisma. If today we read them, it is not for original philosophical or theological insights, but because we sense that (as a considerable philosopher put it) they "really practiced the truth—the faith—in love."

Reading through certain crucial articles that marked Lou Twomey's gargantuan output, I ran into these somewhat cryptic sentences in the last issue of *Social Order* (September, 1963). Captioned "Ave atque Vale," the editorial was a valedictory to the journal's readers. Lou wrote: "It is not that we of the ISO (Institute of Social Order) do not appreciate the critical importance of social action. This field, however, is being serviced by a relatively large number of dedicated clergy and laity, while those engaged in social research are relatively few."

To me Lou had always seemed someone eminently involved in "social action" rather than a researcher. He respected research in other people and was always ready to put it to practical use. On occasion, however, as Father Fichter recalls, he could be impatient with people who wanted to take time out for doctoral degree work, claiming that "there just isn't enough time." Lou appeared rather the platform orator, who would have been eminently at home on London's Hyde Park corner; the master rhetorician, putting debaters' techniques to full use; the artist of the enthymeme, sure of his major premises and conclusions, not always anxious about factual minor premises, which he seemed to leave to scholars to fill in.

Was it simply that *Social Order* had come to a financial impasse? Or did he have second thoughts and wish he had done more of the sort of hard research done by his Mobile counterpart, Albert S. Foley, S.J., or his friend and supporter, Joseph H. Fichter, S.J.? Or did he feel what that unique pioneer, John LaFarge, S.J., emphatically told me to advise younger men aspiring to do interracial work: "Tell them to become serious specialists if they want to do good work!"? I have found no clue in Lou's writings and suspect we shall never know.

The second sentence from "Ave atque Vale" quoted above is also mysterious, at least if taken literally and not merely as a sort of rhetorical sop. Had he found, at last, "a relatively large number of dedicated clergy and laity" involved in social action? Or is the operative word "relatively," and, if so, relative to what? Surely there are no indications anywhere else that he was satisfied or abandoning the "fire that never says 'it is enough'."

I asked Leo Brown why *Social Order* was dropped. He replied: "The Jesuit provincials—some of them, at least—felt that it was a waste of manpower. So did Father Theodore Purcell, the new director, who also wanted the Institute to move to some more obviously important place. Cambridge, Mass., near Harvard, was chosen and the magazine dropped. True, it was an expensive proposition. But I am convinced that it did a job that was needed. It was the one organ on social matters in which serious discussion could be carried on. And the readership, while not large, was very important. It must have been hard for Lou to have to write that farewell note."

Father Purcell recalls that the decision to move to Cambridge came after the decision to close *Social Order* and "after Lou had returned to New Orleans. So, Lou was not really involved in the move to Cambridge. He had done yeoman work for the journal. He, as I recall, was very much a part of all our discussions and decisions and concurred in them. We all felt much regret—but we felt it was for the good— the stress on research."

Lou was disappointed at the tradiness of Catholics generally and many of his brother Jesuits in working for integration. In the *Blueprint* again and again he pointed this out. In the March, 1961, issue, for example he told his conferees: "American Jesuits as a whole have little to pride ourselves on when we examine our attitudes and conduct toward the Negro." He contrasted his Order with the Quakers, the Urban League and the National Association for the Advancement of Colored People, declaring that "humanitarian motivation has elicited in them far greater response to the rights of America's most depressed class than the virtues of justice and charity have in us." He further contrasted the work of the Josephites, members of the Society of the Divine Word, and several other religious groups whose express aim was work for blacks. Meantime, "their resources were too slight and the assistance and sympathy of bishops and of other priests and nuns too little and too late to adequately sustain their courageous efforts."

Here as elsewhere one must keep in mind that Lou Twomey was almost a textbook example of what Max Weber calls the "prophet." As Joseph Fichter put it, "Lou constantly issued 'warnings' and the spell of his thundering oratory was in the deadly serious way he railed at the injustices of our time." For it would be ungracious to suppose that Lou was unaware of the work of other Southern Jesuits in behalf of the rights of black people.

Long before Lou appeared on the scene, for example, Florence Sullivan, S.J., had done courageous pioneer work. Other Southern Jesuits like Cornelius Thenstead and John Henry Millet worked strenuously for many years in impecunious predominantly "black" parishes. Joseph Fichter, as previously mentioned, was doing invaluable scholarly research and was much involved in active programs, strongly supporting Lou's somewhat different approach to the same cause. In varying ways, but effectively, some of Lou's conferees at Loyola were no less conscientiously involved—Jacques E. Yenni, Henry R. Montecino, Alvin J. Pilie, Harold L. Cooper, Guy J. Lemieux, Charles E. O'Neill, Louis J. Hiegel, H. James Yamauchi, and others.

If this were a study of Southern Jesuits and race, several other names would be mentioned. Among the foremost is Albert S. Foley, whose work at Spring Hill College, Mobile, Alabama, in many ways parallels Lou's. In fact, Foley's work in behalf of blacks antedates his friend's. Back in 1946, during an organizational meeting of the South ern ISO (Institute of Social Order) it was agreed that the focus of interracial work for Southern Jesuits would be Foley's Interracial Committee, while Loyola's Industrial Relations Committee would continue to be directed by historian Charles C. Chapman, S.J. This was before Lou returned from his graduate work in St. Louis.

I have gone through minutes of ISO meetings during this early period and studied the correspondence of Foley and Twomey. The two men, while working in somewhat different areas, frequently cooperated—Lou printed articles by Foley and distributed thousands of copies of his leaflet *Black Faced Minstrels: Ten Reasons Why They Are Not So Funny*. An entire volume would be needed to describe Foley's vast enterprise. Something of their differences may be suggested in the following quotation from a recent letter of Foley's: "Lou was doing his thing over there as his conscience guided him and I was pursuing a somewhat different tack over here because I was in an entirely different situation. Lou's approach was mainly through labor relations. To this day I cannot make any progress at all with the labor union people because I have been identified with the blacks and their cause."

During Foley's early work at Spring Hill College, in 1954, president Andrew Cannon Smith, S.J., integrated the college. The local Ku Klux Klan burned a cross on the campus and otherwise harassed the work of Foley. Some years later during a meeting in New York I publicly asked Father Smith how much the integrating of Spring Hill College had cost. He reflected, then replied: "About two buildings." Given the college's financial straits, integration was exceedingly costly.

In an important address to more than 60 Jesuit presidents of universities and colleges (August 5, 1975), Father Pedro Arrupe, superior general of the Society of Jesus, had a great deal to say about the role of "prophet." "Let me make clear what I do not mean, and what I do mean, by that word 'prophetic.'

"I do not mean the angry, facile denunciation of a particular evil. I do not mean a proclamation which, while purporting to liberate the weak and powerless, instigates them to a self-righteous exaltation of their own virtue and to hatred and scorn for those who are not of their number.

"I use the word *prophet* here in a biblical sense: one who is entrusted with a spiritual mission, that of bearing witness to the power and love of God towards men. By *prophetic* I mean the persevering, fearless speaking forth on the issues of the day by people whose views are rooted in Christ's teaching, clarified through discernment with their community, and consistent with their own total dedication to Christ. The prophet 'speaks God's message' (I Cord. 14:24), not only when it is willingly accepted, but also and especially when it is seen as a 'hard saying,' painful to all-too-human ways of viewing what God expects of man in history. The prophet has let himself be steeped in God, with the result that he is free interiorly and pure of heart. He is sympathetically critical of all movements and institutions, many of which are of course excellent, but all of them limited."

On first reading this text (perhaps because I was involved in putting this biography together), I instantly felt that it was almost a description of Lou Twomey.

Too bad Lou didn't live a year longer, to see his Loyola University's College of Arts and Sciences elect a black, Dooky Chase, Jr., as president of the student body. Or a few years longer, to be present in 1974 when the University awarded the Doctorate of Humane Letters to black actress Cicely Tyson, and the following year to musician Mary Lou Williams. In a recent letter Miss Williams recalls: "thirty years ago, when I was with the Kirk Orchestra, we travelled all through Louisiana and it was dreadful; often we didn't eat for days, afraid to stop. Now it seems better than the North. I've never been so happy as recently in New Orleans."

Much of the change was surely owing to Lou Twomey's insistent, energetic work. Even if the following is hyperbolic, as eulogies tend to be, it comes from a judicious person writing Ray Ariatti two years after Lou's death. Federal Judge J. Skelly Wright, who had brought United States law to bear on segregation in New Orleans, had this to say: "In my judgment, Father Twomey contributed more to the advancement of social justice in the New Orleans area than anyone I know. I trust that someone will come along soon to fill the void of his passing." The someone is, of course, Father David A. Boileau.

Everyone closely associated with Lou with whom I have talked speaks of him as the most generous and unselfish person. Somehow, despite an activity that most people would find killing and that psychologists might diagnose as "compulsive," he always seemed available. On Sundays he would often help in parish churches, and, as one who frequently heard him reports, "every sermon was well prepared." As exhausted as he must have often been, his close associate Harold L. Cooper, S.J., recalls, "he way always friendly, always ready to laugh and banter. As solemn as his thoughts were about justice and charity, he was never pedantic. As much as he hated sin—particularly sins of injustice and uncharitableness—he was above hating sinners.

"He saw the *good* in people; he knew, for example that N. was basically a kind person, though the victim of ignorance about how to apply his kindness. When N. referred to Lou as an 'encyclical waver' and 'a raging fanatic,' Lou smiled and would get a laugh out of it when I teased him and called him simply 'Raging.'

"He had three real adversaries among the Loyola Jesuits. To them Lou was a complete *bête noire*. They didn't fear him in the way they feared Joe Fichter. They knew that Lou was not an intellectual, a theoretician. They feared, disliked and avoided him because he actually practiced what he preached. Subconsciously, I feel, they sensed Lou was a reproach, unwittingly to be sure, to them. It was N. who went farthest in that opposition, calling Lou a Communist—and seriously meaning it. Still, Lou felt no personal animosity. He was not the subjectivist that many ardent men can be."

This, so far as I can ascertain, is the basis of a myth sometimes heard that Lou was not accepted by the Loyola Jesuit community. By the time I was assigned to Loyola (though I had often visited there previously), in 1958, the three men mentioned by Father Cooper were either dead or so aged as to be ineffectual. Everyone else, so far as I could judge, held him in real esteem and affection. There was always a great deal of banter, to be sure, such as always surrounds exciting people, but it seemed to be centered in genuine friendship.

If Lou felt somewhat lacking in the degree of support that his causes merited, it was partly because his zeal was insatiable. Almost to a man, his peers were at least sympathetic to his aims, and those of us slightly younger (I recall a dozen or so) felt perhaps more of of the sway of his charismatic personality. Part of the antipathy of the three elders mentioned above may have arisen from their awareness that he was a powerful influence on the next generation, hence the future. If they thought this they were right; the future was his.

To be sure, he always felt that not enough money was provided for his work. It never is. Universities generally, and notably Loyola during Lou's early years there, operate on tight budgets and normally "in the red." Budget committees tend to allocate funds not so much on the objective worth of a department (whatever that may be or seem to be), but with some relationship to the amount of money the department brings in. In the 1940's grants were rare, even for worthwhile social ventures. (Even later, when dean of the College of Music I recall having to raise money personally to launch a program in liturgical music. The university budget simply could not provide for such an innovation).

Whether or not Lou ever made this explicit, he surely realized that the shockingly modest facilities Loyola gave him at the outset were better than nothing, and that the room and board and other necessities provided him, even when his work could not bring in a cent, were incalculably valuable. So far as we know, he was never tempted to leave Loyola. Further, his academic position in a university and his status as Regent of the School of Law vastly enhanced the podium from which he spoke; he never failed to use these to best advantage.

Chapter 7
DEATH

During the last year of his life he had a full-time Jesuit assistant, Francis E. Renfroe. In a recent letter Frank recalls: "Lou had gone down terribly. You recall having supper with us when you discovered how Lou's mind had deteriorated—worrying about things which showed mental instability. Lou suffered terribly. Perhaps his fears were due to an over-strict Jansenistic upbringing. I feel they were tied up with an unwillingness to die at that time. He fought for life almost to the end. I remember when I was crying aloud Lou opened his eyes and looked at me surprised, as if trying to say: 'Are you crying for me?' Lou lived on love. He never ceased to love, no matter who you were, as you well know. He had special love for God's little ones. This was his greatest charisma—his boundless love for the neglected. What a beautiful person! What struck me most about him was his innate ability to make everyone he met realize he was loved by him. You felt that. My regret is that I only came to really know him after his best years of service were at an end. No, they're really not at an end."

This from a person closely associated with him during the months of decline. What is exceptional about Lou Twomey is that an anthology of such tributes, even years after his death, could easily be collected. Gathering data for his biography, both of us have heard the same account with almost phonographic redundancy, a redundancy that might prove cloying to strangers but is totally unsurprising to all who knew Lou well. One final anecdote is only typical. Not long before he died he met a student on campus. "I know you, son . . . Wait, your name is Gaudet. Is your first name Bill?" Gaudet assures me they had met only once before, some five years earlier.

Dr. John Ruli, who was Lou's physician for the last four or five years of his life, tells me that he died of severe, progressive "obstructive emphysema." Lou was, as all his friends recall, an obsessive compulsive smoker. This he explained, recalls Dr. Ruli, in terms of anxiety: "If only I didn't worry so much, Doc." Dr. Ruli remembers

Father Twomey, approximately 1968

Lou as "one of the finest persons I've met in my whole life," but one who seemed to lack confidence in himself. "He seemed to need reassurance. I remember visiting him shortly before he died. He said: 'Doc, a few minutes ago my whole life flashed in front of me in an instant.' 'I'm sure it was a good life,' volunteered Dr. Ruli. 'Gee whiz, Doc, you don't know how much it means to me for you to say that!' "

It was always puzzling to Lou's close friends that such an austere person, generally so demanding of himself, could not "kick" the smoking habit even when he knew he had emphysema. For some years, in fact, he had quit carrying cigarettes. Yet, again and again he would ask friends for them. Not long before he went definitively to the hospital, he walked over with a friend to see a Saints football game—a rare case of self-indulgence. On the way he had to stop several times to catch his breath. But he went on smoking, and the flaw would prove fatal.

To person after person visiting him in the hospital he would say: "Lord, how I regret the day I took that first cigarette!"

Among the ceaseless stream of visitors to the hospital were many of the labor leaders with whom he had worked so faithfully. At his side, as constantly as human endurance could manage, was his devoted friend and intimate associate Ray Ariatti, long deeply involved in trade unionism and the cause of labor. Ray had know Lou since 1950 and had worked in the Institute since 1960.

On one occasion, when the president of Loyola, Homer R. Jolley, visited the hospital, Lou spontaneously made this request: "Take good care of Ray." Ray continues to be employed in the Institute of Human Relations. He has been tirelessly helpful in providing material for this book.

The day before Lou died, October 8, just three days after his 64th birthday, Ariatti was at his bedside in Mercy hospital. Coming in and out of consciousness, Lou turned toward him gasping words that Ray had trouble piecing together.

Just audibly, as Ray recalls, Lou whispered: "We . . . must establish our identity . . . in togetherness . . . (a long hard gasp for breath) . . . toward . . ."

Ray asked: "The social apostolate, Father?"

Lou's lips moved, but there was no sound.

Ray tried again: "Toward the dignity of the human person, Father?"

Lou smiled, nodded and whispered: "Yes."

During those last days in the hospital Lou was constantly gasping for breath and often heard praying aloud: "All for Thee."

Sister Irene Broussard, R.S.M., like Lou a graduate of Loyola (as she likes to say), was with him a great deal of the time. Two Jesuits from Loyola were there all the time, in four or five hour shifts.

Lou knew he was dying and was concerned about the timing of his death. He was anxious not to die on October 7, since Sister Irene was celebrating her 50th anniversary as a nun. He told her several times that he didn't want to spoil her jubilee.

On October 7, despite the celebrations, Sister Irene managed to spend a good deal of time with him, praying for him.

Toward the end of the day Lou laboriously asked: "Are you Sister Irene?"

"Yes, Lou, why do you ask?"

"Because . . . the texture . . . of your sleeve . . . isn't the same." Obviously he could no longer see.

"That's because I just came from chapel, son. We wear a different outfit there. I'll be back in my regular nursing outfit."

She went to her room to change garbs. A summons came: "Hurry to Father Twomey's room, Sister."

It was well after midnight. Lou was struggling for breath. The jubilee day was over. Ray Ariatti was, of course, there. So were two Loyola friends, Fathers Charles O'Neill and Joseph Molloy.

As they were praying, Lou died at 12:58 on the morning of October 8. Sister Irene adds, "calmly and peacefully."

Afterword

In 2017, the Twomey Center for Peace through Justice—the name by which Father Twomey's Institute of Social Order had been known for at least a decade—was closed as part of the financial belt-tightening at Loyola University New Orleans. The directors of the institute or center during its lifetime were:

Rev. Louis J. Twomey, S.J.	1947–1969
Rev. Francis E. Renfroe, S.J.	1969–1970
Rev. David Boileau	1970–1979
Rev. George F. Lundy, S.J.	1980–1986
Theodore A. Quant	1987–1988
David M. Marr	1988–1990
Theodore A. Quant	1990–2013
Dr. Alvaro B. Alcazar	2013–2017

Despite the closure of the Institute, Father Twomey's influence has continued on Jesuits and many others into the present moment. As a high school sophomore, my initial baptism-in-Twomey-fire was at the Summer School of Catholic Action (SSCA) in Dallas in 1961, where I took three multi-day courses from Lou, one on racism, the second on anti-communism, and the third on Catholic Social Teaching. For years afterwards I took advantage of the "For the Asking" section of Lou's *Blueprint* and my free copies of social encyclicals like *Rerum Novarum, Quadragesimo Anno, Mater et Magistra,* and *Pacem in Terris* all still bear the stamp "Institute of Social Order."

I remember all too well the initial meeting of about thirty Jesuit priests and scholastics of the New Orleans Province at the Institute on Easter night and Easter Monday of 1969. A small planning group had asked

Lou to host us to promote Vatican II's vision of social justice and Father Arrupe's 1967 letter to U.S. Jesuits on the Interracial Apostolate. There was a poignancy in air that Easter evening as Lou gave the invocation and gung-ho opening remarks and then left us alone as he prepared to go to Baton Rouge for testimony at the Legislature in the morning. It was as if he passed the torch to us to carry it into the future and then assumed he had done his job. He was dead six months later.

Fred Kammer, S.J., Director
Jesuit Social Research Institute
Loyola University New Orleans
July 31, 2021

Printed by Libri Plureos GmbH in Hamburg, Germany